Praise f

M000308693

I wish I'd had this book at the beginning of my journey and I'm sure it'll resonate with all aspiring female entrepreneurs. It is jam-packed with practical advice and inspiring case studies – a must-read!
SAASHA CELESTIAL-ONE, CO-FOUNDER AND CHIEF OPERATIONS OFFICER, OLIO

Essential for any aspiring entrepreneur. *She Made It* empowers people to take the plunge but also deals with the real challenges entrepreneurship brings.
DAN MURRAY-SERTER, CO-FOUNDER, HEIGHTS; AND HOST, *SECRET LEADERS* PODCAST

A much-needed guide that will empower so many women.
SHAHROO IZADI, BESTSELLING AUTHOR, *THE KINDNESS METHOD* AND *THE LAST DIET*

The ultimate handbook for any aspiring entrepreneur – *She Made It* is smart, accessible and the perfect first step for any woman wanting to run her own business.
REBECCA REID, FORMER DIGITAL EDITOR, *GRAZIA*; AND AUTHOR, *PERFECT LIARS* AND *THE POWER OF RUDE*

Practical and inspirational in equal measure – *She Made It* is packed full of advice, inspiration and wisdom from not just Angelica Malin, but many successful female entrepreneurs. This is a must-read, must-use toolkit for the next generation of kickass female founders and business leaders.
KATIE VANNECK-SMITH, CO-FOUNDER AND PUBLISHER, TORTOISE MEDIA

This is the guide every female entrepreneur needs when starting out. Angelica Malin demystifies what is really involved in starting your business and what it takes to succeed – all the things I wish I'd known beforehand!

STEPHANIE JOHNSON, FOUNDER AND CO-CHIEF EXECUTIVE OFFICER, POLLEN + GRACE

This is the book I wish I'd had when I was getting started. It's absolutely comprehensive, practical, no-nonsense – and truly inspirational! As a reader, you are taken deep beneath the surface, emerging with a clear idea not just of what to do with your life, but why.

RACHEL CARRELL, FOUNDER AND CHIEF EXECUTIVE OFFICER, KORU KIDS

Jam-packed with practical information and actionable tips. The ultimate toolkit for women who want to take control of their career.

ZANNA VAN DIJK, INFLUENCER AND CO-FOUNDER, STAY WILD SWIM

The book I wish I'd had when starting my business. It covers all areas you need to mentally prepare yourself and your business for success. All female entrepreneurs – new and experienced – can take what they need from *She Made It*.

LUCY HITCHCOCK, FOUNDER, SASSY DIGITAL AND PARTNER IN WINE

A vital toolkit for any founder looking to build a structurally sound business, *She Made It* leverages decades of combined entrepreneurial learnings to ensure that 'learning the hard way' becomes a concept of the past.

GABRIELA HERSHAM, CO-FOUNDER AND CHIEF EXECUTIVE OFFICER, HUCKLETREE

It's such an exciting time for female entrepreneurs and this book really helps demystify the process of launching your own business, with lots of great actionable tips and real-life examples. A must-read for any woman wanting to start their own business – your toolkit for success in 2021!

CAMILLA AINSWORTH, FOUNDER AND CHIEF EXECUTIVE OFFICER, M+LKPLUS

She Made It

She Made It

*The toolkit for female founders in
the digital age*

Angelica Malin

KoganPage

Publisher's note
Every possible effort has been made to ensure that the information contained in this book is accurate at the time of going to press, and the publisher and author cannot accept responsibility for any errors or omissions, however caused. No responsibility for loss or damage occasioned to any person acting, or refraining from action, as a result of the material in this publication can be accepted by the editor, the publisher or the author.

First published in Great Britain and the United States in 2021 by Kogan Page Limited

2nd Floor, 45 Gee Street	122 W 27th St, 10th Floor	4737/23 Ansari Road
London	New York, NY 10001	Daryaganj
EC1V 3RS	USA	New Delhi 110002
United Kingdom		India

www.koganpage.com

Kogan Page books are printed on paper from sustainable forests.

ISBNs

Hardback	978 1 78966 686 1
Paperback	978 1 78966 684 7
eBook	978 1 78966 685 4

British Library Cataloguing-in-Publication Data

A CIP record for this book is available from the British Library.

Library of Congress Cataloging-in-Publication Data

Library of Congress Cataloging-in-Publication Data is available. Control Number: 2020047898

Typeset by Integra Software Services, Pondicherry
Print production managed by Jellyfish
Printed and bound by CPI Group (UK) Ltd, Croydon CR0 4YY

For my mum, who taught me the meaning of a strong woman

Contents

Preface

What if I told you that time is how you spend your love? That every moment of your working day has the ability to be an expression of joy, creativity and fulfilment? That you can wake up feeling fired up and excited for the day ahead? That you don't have to slog it out in a job you don't love? That you can do anything you want to do? And you can start today.

Once upon a time, we were led to believe that a job is something that exists within the hours of 9 to 5, something you do to survive, and hell, if you're lucky enough to enjoy it, then that's a bonus. For my parents' generation, work was a very different thing. The focus was not on loving your work, being fulfilled by it or bringing about change in the world, but getting the job done, paying the bills and, basically, settling. Settling for 'good enough'. Settling for an ordinary job, an ordinary life, 2.5 kids and a mortgage, if you're lucky. But things are shifting in the modern workplace.

I'm here to tell you that things are changing, especially for women. Female entrepreneurs are rising through the ranks at a rate like never before. Women are sick of the structures in place that are holding them back – be it the traditional career ladder, inflexible workplaces or toxic corporate culture – and are waking up to their own potential. Throughout the UK, a huge awakening is happening for womankind: more women than ever before are committing to designing a career – and a life – that they love. Are you going to join them?

There are more female entrepreneurs in the UK now than ever before – at last count, 1.5 million women in the UK are opting to be self-employed. Female entrepreneurship is booming, but not quickly enough – in the 2019 Alison Rose Female Entrepreneurship Review, it was revealed that only one in three entrepreneurs in the UK are female, a gender gap amounting to 1.1 million businesses. And investing in women pays – according to the same review, up to £250 billion of new value could be added to the UK economy if women started and scaled new businesses at the same rate as the UK.[1]

Women are done with stuffy work cultures; I've seen a monumental shift in beliefs around work, with thousands of women opting to be their own boss, work flexibly and create a career they love. Purpose over profit: the focus for women today is on fulfilment, flexibility and fun in their careers.

I believe that you can 'have it all', because the meaning of having it all has changed for the modern woman. Success no longer means a high-flying corporate career, an expense account and liquid lunches. It means believing in the work you're doing, having *impact* and forging your own path. As you'll see in the many inspiring case studies ahead, the focus is away from purely financial success, but personal growth through work – creating companies that are impactful, challenging and change-driven.

But let us remember that success is personal. Success will look and feel different for every woman. You don't need to have kids if it doesn't suit you. You don't have to stay in a job that you don't love. You don't have to work for someone else. You don't have to worry about the relentless juggle of work and family life. You can make work, work for you.

Why the shift towards self-employment for women? For one, the internet has created so many new opportunities to explore entrepreneurship, providing myriad possibilities through the touch of a button. Never before have we had access to such amazing free marketing tools, where we can build, engage and, ultimately, monetize online audiences. Everything you need to help your business flourish is right in front of you: you just need to open up that laptop and get going.

I really do believe that amazing things happen when women support each other. Women supporting women is more than just a cute phrase used by athleisure brands to sell leggings – sisterhood is real, and it's manifested in the pages of this book. I've met some incredible women through my personal business journey, and now they are going to help to support, advise and mentor you too.

Everything I've learned, everyone I've met, every mistake I've made, is penned in the pages of this book – I hope it will help inspire you to take a leap into the unknown and find a career that sets your soul on fire. Because I believe in you and I know you're going to do big things in this life.

Acknowledgements

Writing a book takes an army, and I'm so grateful for all the wonderful people in my life who have helped, supported and advised me through this time. My editor Geraldine at Kogan Page, who helped me bring this book to life, despite the challenging circumstances of a global pandemic and emergency surgery. Even in the most unexpected circumstances, your positivity, resilience and belief in me has been truly inspiring.

To the incredible women who raise me up daily – Gemma, Claude, Rebecca, Lucy and Rose – you have redefined sisterhood to me and showed me the power of female friendships through the toughest times. To my amazing family – Howard, James and Oliver – for your unwavering support through many a business meltdown.

Behind every strong woman is an even stronger mother pushing her on. To my incredible mother Suzi – my best friend – and my grandmother Elizabeth – the ultimate matriarch – who taught me from a young age that all a woman really needs in life is self-belief, confidence and a good cup of tea.

And finally, obviously, to a shout out to Taylor Swift, without whom there would probably be no book at all.

Introduction

I'm Angelica Malin – Founder and Editor-in-Chief at About Time Magazine, one of the UK's leading lifestyle platforms. I also host #SheStartedIt LIVE, our amazing female empowerment festivals in London, and #SheStartedIt podcast, where I interview incredible female entrepreneurs. I live the multi-hyphen life – each day is different, from moderating events to hosting podcasts, writing features and working on commercial strategy. But what ties everything together for me is a genuine belief in female potential; from events to editorial, female empowerment runs through the veins of my business and life.

I did not, shall we say, 'decide' to be an entrepreneur. In fact, I didn't have a plan at all. My CV, should I ever need to write one, would be woefully short: I've had four proper jobs in my life, two of which I was fired from. My most flamboyant exit, a few months after leaving university, was particularly character-forming – I worked at a brilliant magazine, which I loved very much, and I thought I would be there for many years to come. But the job was short-lived (apparently I was too entrepreneurial for it!) and I cried for weeks afterwards, feeling like my whole world had come crashing down. With hindsight, I can now see that being fired was one of the best things to ever happen to me. Perhaps that's why they call it getting fired – it certainly put fire in my belly and pushed me to make something of my career. Sometimes, our hardest experiences are what motivate us – we must be grateful for them.

So, here I was, fresh out of university in the summer of 2013, with six months of real-world experience under my belt, and I was faced with one of the most common graduate problems: 'what now?' There's no clear answer for that, but if you're struggling, I would suggest trying to connect with your instinct and intuition. For example, I had no idea what I wanted to do with my career, but whilst at university, I'd had a brief fling with being a cake maker, starting a small business with my best friend supplying cakes to the local cafes in Bristol. Whilst there was a fundamental flaw in the business (we couldn't bake), it taught me a huge amount about sales, branding and the power of face-to-face contact with your consumers.

I also learned that I relished the challenge of being self-employed, the journey of taking an idea into action. Following a feeling can be very useful when you're faced with what to do with your life. I followed the feeling of fulfilment in being self-employed and it led me down this amazing path.

There was no 'aha' moment for About Time; it was much more of a slow burn – a business that forms and crystallizes over time, revealing itself piece by piece. The notion that an idea just comes to you like a lightning bolt is somewhat pressuring. Don't be afraid of starting with a hint of an idea. Some business ideas are big and ambitious (usually the ones that need the most start-up capital), and others are modest and become more defined over time. It's okay to start small, grow day-by-day, rather than trying to take the world by storm overnight. Sometimes an idea doesn't even need to be new; you just have to do something in a fresh, interesting way.

How did my idea happen? Well, whilst working at the previous magazine, I spent a lot time online researching features for a food column. I realized that most of the London-focused online magazines were not providing the content I was looking for. I searched and searched, trying to find good, curated online guides to London, and nothing quite hit the spot. Sure, there were big magazines like *Time Out*, the *Evening Standard* and the *Telegraph*, which provided lots of massive guides and endlessly long lists, but nothing which felt, well, personal. Nothing felt authentic, like I knew the person behind the writing and trusted them.

Frankly, nothing felt bossy enough. I was sick of scrolling through super-long lists of recommendations – I was time-poor and wanted to be told where, in this moment, was worth my time and money in London. And thus, the idea for About Time came about – someone who told you 'This, it's about time you did this one thing' – with the authority and trust of someone you really knew. Like a friend in the know, who tips you off about something great, that's how the idea for the website began.

So not a light-bulb moment, but a small seed of an idea, a frustration, that could be channelled into something positive and solutions-focused. The website was both about time, in the sense that time is the most precious commodity we have (and yet we don't treat it with anywhere near the same amount of respect as our stuff), and literally about time, because nothing like it quite existed.

So, I set about creating the best lifestyle website in the UK. When I think back to those early days in 2013, I really didn't know what I was doing, but I had belief in an idea, which is the most important thing. Belief is what will get you through the hard days, because, boy, there are going to be those. And I had a real sense of self-confidence. I don't remember even entertaining the idea that the website would fail, or that no one would read it. I just believed blindly, wildly, in what I was doing.

I was so caught up in the concept, the launch and the magazine that I didn't allow failure to enter my mindset, which, now, with hindsight and having read dozens of self-help books, is exactly what you're meant to do. Sometimes we can freak ourselves out with the idea of launching, trying to perfect something too much, writing business plans, spreadsheets and targets, that we can lose track of the thing that excited us in the first place. I can't stress this enough: sometimes you just have to *do*. Sure, get all the experience you can, speak to people, take courses, read books, but sometimes the best way to get something off the ground isn't to plan; it's just to do and learn on the job. Baptism of fire, learning by and through our mistakes, that's the way we grow.

So, at the end of 2013, I put everything in motion – I found a freelance web designer, worked with him remotely to create a website with the right aesthetic, and brought together a group of inspiring young lifestyle writers to provide content. I found an inexpensive graphic designer to design us a logo, got a photographer friend to take some professional snaps of me, and in March 2014, a very much first-time entrepreneur, I took the very first version of About Time live. All in all, the website cost us £500 – a real business on a shoestring. To put that into perspective, our second website in 2015, a design update, cost £5,000, and our next one will cost in the region of £10,000. Remember: it's okay to start small and grow at a rate that feels comfortable to you.

We launched the website in early March 2014, and on its first day, it had 12,000 users on the site. I say we, out of habit, but it was really just me, one girl behind something that looked much bigger. It was an incredible response – I'd had blogs in the past, but nothing of this reach – and I knew on that day that there was something there, I just had to harness it. If you're wondering where a lot of that traffic came from, I'd been slowly building up my social following at the previous magazine, with a few thousand followers on Twitter at that point – not a lot, but enough to give any new project a boost. Around 70 per cent of the traffic that day was from Twitter, and to this day not a lot has changed on that front – we still get a huge amount of our traffic from social media.

But that was launch day. Day two looked very different. I spent the whole day panicking – sitting in my pyjamas, in my childhood bedroom, wondering what on earth to do next. I remember crying my eyes out, realizing that I knew how to launch the thing but had absolutely no idea how to run it. Learning how to run a content-based business, keeping it fresh and interesting, is one of the biggest challenges facing anyone in the online space – and something I can't wait to teach you in this book.

So how I got the magazine through that first year – and grew our audience to over 95,000 users a month in 205 countries, and over 100,000 social followers, with over 90 writers and a growing team in London – will be revealed in these pages. Anyone who tells you that you can't do a job that's fun is telling themselves a lie. I'm here to tell you that you can have a career that you wake up excited about, each and every day, and I've enlisted the help of some fellow female entrepreneurs along the way to share their insights into building businesses they love. That's my story; now it's time to write yours.

How to read this book

This book is a little bit of everything; advice, case studies and workbook, it's a mix of the personal and the practical. Because, as much as this book is about me and the amazing female entrepreneurs I've met along the way, it is also about **you**.

Each chapter addresses a theme within the entrepreneurial landscape, from understanding your digital brand to building a team – I wanted to bring a range of voices into the book, so I've enlisted the help of some incredible female entrepreneurs to share their personal insights. If you've ever wondered to yourself, 'how did she make it?', then this is your chance to find out.

I'm all about action. You can read all the advice you like, but unless you can create some actionable steps to understand your plan going forward, and actually *do* the thing, it's pretty useless. This is a book about doing, not just learning. Thus, mostly at/ towards the end of each chapter, you'll find a workbook with some questions to ask yourself. I would recommend reading the book as a whole, and then coming back chapter by chapter to fill in the workbook, as you may find thoughts crystallizing as you make your way through the book. But, you do you. If you feel like answering every chapter as you go, then go for it!

Don't be afraid to decorate the pages with your own thoughts and ideas throughout – I'd recommend reading with a high-lighter and pencil, so you can annotate as you go. Bring the book alive and make it your own – nothing brings me more joy than the idea of the book filled with life, colour and ideas.

PART ONE

All about you

CHAPTER ONE

How to own your career

If you cannot name your dreams, you cannot fulfil them.

The primary product of a business is, and always will be, you. Let's start by discovering more about *you* – your goals, ambitions and the kind of founder you want to be. So often, I find, women focus on the product they want to create, but forget to ask crucial questions about themselves. Find a business style that suits your personality; we forget that, at the end of it all, we are our business.

Women often struggle to articulate their ambitions, experiencing self-doubt and low confidence when it comes to starting their own business. I've hosted dozens of talks to roomfuls of women where they've gingerly held up their hand at the end and asked: 'But how do I believe in myself more?'

We have more barriers to overcome, perhaps, in living boldly and bravely with our business. I personally grew up in a male-dominated school environment where 'CEO' was seen as a typically male role, and girls were encouraged to pursue degrees in the arts, over business or science. Things are changing, but I still think we have some catching up to do in terms of confidence and self-belief. So, let's begin the journey by examining your own personal ambitions.

It all starts by looking inside and being honest with yourself. When it comes to business, I am a slow, steady and sustainable person. I like to do things step-by-step, building my business one day at a time, and allowing the bigger picture to gradually present itself. I can be easily overwhelmed by rushing into decisions, taking on too much commitment or having big financial pressure. Understanding this helps shape the business I run.

I know, in my heart of hearts, that running a huge company with offices all over the globe, a massive payroll and a board of directors wouldn't be right for me. I like to keep things flexible and scalable, allowing my business to work around my lifestyle and priorities. If it means working in a lovely co-working space, with a team of five people and part-time assistance I can pull in when needed, then that works for me. Don't be afraid of doing business in your own terms. Don't let other people's definition of success affect yours. There's no singular, right way to do business.

In business, we're often sold on the concept of 'hard' expansion – going global, million-pound profit or an aggressive exit strategy – but, as you'll see in the case studies ahead, business can often start small. There's a softer side; one that's about creating a business that works around your life, gives you deep fulfilment and a sense of purpose. Ultimately, the reason for starting your own business is to create something that you connect with on a deeper level, that you can pour your heart, soul and creativity into.

So, work out what kind of founder you want to be – do you dream of having a six-figure business? Do you want to be able to work from home? Do you want to have a job where you can walk the dog during the day? Get specific about your dreams. Let them live and breathe through you.

Don't get me wrong, none of this is easy. Learning how to focus your energy, refine your concept and articulate your vision takes lots of introspection. Let's unpack some of your personal desires when it comes to building your business. I'm going to help you iron out some questions before launching your own venture. It's time to grab a pen and paper and dig deep.

Visualizing your future

Everyone's business vision will be different. It all depends on your personal desires and the kind of company you see yourself running.

Let's start by playing a game – take a few minutes for the below:

Shut your eyes and imagine the perfect work day in your life. What does it look like?

Where are you working – is it a big glass office in central London, are you working from home in your comfiest clothes? How many people are with you? What's the content of your day? What does your working day look like? What kind of tasks are you doing?

Positive visualization is powerful – if we can't see our dreams, then we can't achieve them. Make your dream technicolour in your head. Let the future you become hyper-realistic. Imagine your future life in bright colour and 4D clarity, as if watching it on a big screen. This is the film of your life, and you're the main star in it.

You might not get there overnight. You might not get there at all. But the point is, by getting clear about what your perfect work setup looks like, you'll start making changes in your life to get closer to that point, every day. You won't even have to work at it that hard; you'll just connect more with your intuition and feel what's right in your gut. That's the beauty of having dreams – they're there to guide you.

Women can often lack the confidence to name their dreams. Imposter syndrome – defined as a mixture of anxiety and persistent inability to recognize one's own success – is high among women. A recent NatWest campaign found that 60 per cent of women dreamed of starting their own business but didn't have the confidence to start.[1] Launching your own business begins by giving yourself permission to dream big. As women, we can often hold ourselves back, living with limiting beliefs that we're not capable, don't have enough knowledge or aren't ready to take the plunge. Let's be honest: the perfect time was probably yesterday, so you might as well start today.

During the course of this book, I want you to get into the habit of day-dreaming. You might be surprised what your subconscious throws up when you allow yourself to. Next time you're on your morning commute, before putting on music or scrolling through Instagram, take a moment to pause.

Are you blocking your thoughts from being heard? Are you trying to drown yourself out with distractions? Instead of filling your mind with other things, just let it wander. Get comfortable with silence. Guide them, listen to them. You'll be amazed how clear your thoughts are when you allow them to come to the surface.

In the next chapter, we'll be looking at ways you can form the building blocks of your dream career, from thoughts to action. First, take a few moments to answer the following questions and be as honest as possible when answering.

WORKBOOK

Q1: When you get really clear about your dreams, what do they look like?

_____
_____
_____
_____

Q2: Where do you get your energy from? What makes you feel most alive?

_____
_____
_____
_____

Q3: What does your ideal day at work look like? Imagine it in technicolour.

_____
_____
_____
_____

Q4: What kind of company do you see yourself running? What company size, location and culture?

_____
_____
_____
_____
_____

Q5: What's stopping you from pursuing that dream? Name three things you feel are in your way.

_____
_____
_____
_____

CASE STUDY   She Made It: Tania Boler

Name: Tania Boler
Job title: Founder and CEO of Elvie

How did the idea for your business come about?

After years of working for the UN and Marie Stopes, I considered myself to be an expert on the subject of sexual health. But when I became pregnant, I realized I knew far less about my own body than I ought to, especially about my pelvic floor.

These muscles, which lie underneath the pelvis, undergo a huge amount of strain throughout pregnancy, childbirth and menopause. After delving into the world of pelvic floor rehabilitation through exercise, I discovered the complete lack of innovation within the women's health tech space to address the issue. It became clear to me that technology was the tool with which we could make Kegel training more accessible to women all over the world.

There was a clear opportunity here to design and create a luxurious, innovative product that was both addressing a major issue and providing an entertaining experience. This ultimately drove me to create the Elvie Trainer and work to de-stigmatize topics surrounding women's health closer to home.

How long did it take you to launch it?

Elvie was founded in 2013. Our flagship product, Elvie Trainer, was brought to market in under two years, launching in autumn 2015. This is quite fast for a hardware product of this nature, especially with the level of complexity involved with the Trainer.

What are the practical steps you took to launch the business?

↳ Building the team

The first step was building a small but nimble team of world-class designers and engineers right from the outset. From three of us on day one, to six when the product went to launch.

Getting Alexander Asseily on board, first as an investor and then as a business partner, was a key step in launching Elvie. He had experience building a billion-dollar business in the US and encouraged me not to bootstrap but instead raise more money and hire great talent right from the start.

↳ Gathering the funds

Investment rounds can be gruelling and feel like an uphill struggle. After Alex Asseily's investment, a defining moment in driving the launch of Elvie was the grant we received from Innovate UK. It enabled us to start from scratch to find the perfect-shaped product that women would love to use.

↳ Building the prototype

We found that R&D processes were very costly, so we decided to invest much more up front in user research. We started with a blank canvas, getting over 150 women to test seven different shapes and iterations of the product.

We found there was very little data or research on the vagina as a part of anatomy, so we brought in a talented head designer, John O'Toole from Dyson, who developed the prototype for Elvie Trainer, remodelling it based on the live feedback we were getting.

We wanted to ensure this close attention to detail was there from the word 'go'. This is what has set the precedent for Elvie creating its world-class products.

What's the biggest learning curve you've had with Elvie?

Definitely the process of managing a tech firm as a non-tech founder. Specifically, the process of hiring the right talent and managing those teams when, at the time, I didn't know my software from my firmware. I definitely got some things wrong at the beginning, one of those being to hire engineering graduates instead of investing in more experienced engineers. Bringing in the experienced Alex Asseily as an adviser really sped up the learning process in this department.

How did you finance the business to get it off the ground?

I had applied for an Innovate UK competition and, to my surprise, won – that was one of the most exhilarating days of my life.

The next stage was through angel investors. Responses were varied and it took a while to break through. I found that the investors only took meetings if they were truly interested, so the success rate once I was able to get in a room with them was high.

We raised Series A funding from our first institutional investor, Octopus. I chose them partly because of Simon King, the partner, who I felt really understood our values and was just generally someone I could trust.

The Series B funding round secured us $42 million – the largest investment received by a fem-tech company to date.

What were the biggest challenges around raising investment?

When simply bringing up the word 'vagina' in initial meetings raised eyebrows, you can imagine that contending with majority male tech investors was a big challenge to contend with. I heavily relied on numbers to win people over, placing a large emphasis on how neglected areas equal opportunity.

Any tips for budding entrepreneurs looking to raise capital?

Basically, do your homework. You need to work with this person for five to seven years, so make sure it is the right match. For the Series B funding round, for example, I insisted on having lunch with the partner to get to know him outside a formal panel meeting.

Some investors can be really pushy. I have turned down companies that we had ethical questions about – it's not worth compromising your mission.

If you could do your investment round again, what would you do differently?

It's always best to ask for more money than you think you'll need. It puts you in a stronger position to ask for more and negotiate down than having to ask for more later down the line.

What are your five top tips for aspiring female entrepreneurs?

⤷ **Find a network** – Having a group of like-minded people to learn and share ideas within the industry will be key to providing support when times are tough. If finding a network is proving challenging, build your own!

⤷ **Develop rhino-thick skin** – Rejection is part of the game. But the good news is that with rejection comes resilience. You have to focus on the end goal, learn not to care too much about what other people think and find the silver lining.

↪ **Bring the swagger** – Confidence is key. Even if you don't have all the answers, a sprinkle of the 'fake it until you make it' attitude goes a long way. If you believe in your mission enough, other people will believe in it too.

↪ **Take risks** – Don't be afraid to bring something completely new to the table. To bring about real change, you have to be willing to do something no one else will. This inevitably comes with some risk, but it's the kind that is worth taking.

↪ **Believe in the mission** – If you have a strong belief in what your business is trying to achieve and why it is needed, everything falls into place. Keep your mission clear and concise and make it your north star!

CHAPTER TWO

How to build a business you love

Now, the fun bit: the chance to build a business you love. To me, this is where your creativity and personality can shine through. Your business is a blank slate, ready to be filled with colour, life and vibrancy.

We're going to connect with your passion and creativity in this chapter. I'm sure there are dozens of business books (mostly written by men!) out there who will tell you how to build a business using spreadsheets and projections. I'm afraid that's not this book. This is about building a company – and career – that has longevity, one that you love, which goes beyond simply paying the bills (although it's going to do that too). Let's create a business that comes from a place of purpose, something that you wake up excited about each and every day.

Why is passion so important? Well, passion makes everything else flow. Estée Lauder is one of my business heroes, who built a global multi-million-pound company from the kitchen table. In a TV documentary on her in 1987, *Estée Lauder: The Sweet Smell of Success*, she talked about belief and sales:

I have never worked a day in my life without selling. If I believe in something, I sell it and I sell it hard.[1]

Find the passion, and the sales will follow

The bad news is there are no shortcuts to building a company of this kind. It's a step-by-step process, and you'll probably have to change direction a few times to get it right. Building a business of this kind is gradual, with a lot of hard graft along the way. The good news is, you're going to feel more alive and fired up than ever before.

Honestly, you can't run a business without passion. It's what gives any business longevity, because passion will carry you through when times are tough. There's going to be so many moments when you think to yourself, 'What on earth am I doing?' and, in those moments of self-doubt, passion and purpose are what will keep you going. Passion is a grounding emotion – it's what will guide you back time and time again.

Passion is particularly relevant for female founders. Dozens of female founders I've interviewed over the years have found business inspiration in a problem or challenge they've faced – led by passion. Tania Boler, for example – the Founder of Elvie, a fem-tech company that recently raised $42 million Series B funding, and who we met just in the last chapter – started her business as a passion project out of the experience of mother-hood. Many female-founded businesses in the UK are born out of personal experience – whether that's driven by motherhood, a frustration in society, a kitchen-table hobby – and have gone on to be the foundation for their work. If you're looking for busi-ness ideas, look within your own life for inspiration.

TOP TIPS: FINDING BUSINESS INSPIRATION

Want to start your own business but stuck for inspiration? Here are some top tips for connecting with the world around you for ideas:

↳ Are there conversations which you hear time and time again amongst friends or colleagues? Perhaps a particular frustration in their lives which could be a starting point for a business?

↳ Is there something you find personally frustrating, which you wish someone could fix?

↳ Have you been inspired by anything you've seen in other countries, which you'd love to bring to your country?

↳ Have you ever used a company or service and thought, 'I could do that better'? If so, what? How would you improve upon the current offering?

↳ Is there a product in the market that you think really needs a refresh? Perhaps you don't need to invent something new but could make it fresh and interesting and appeal to a different market.

Before we move on to the mechanics and marketing of your business, we need to figure out your *why*. Use this chapter of the book as your personal workbook for figuring out your motivation for launching a business. Even if it changes over time (which it will!), it's a great idea to have a *why* as a starting point.

Figuring out your *why*

It's important to know the *why* for your work personally, as well as for any business you launch. The stronger you feel about the vision and values for your career, the more guidance you'll have on future ventures – I see a why as an anchor and something you can return to when feeling lost. Here are some things to consider:

↪ What values are important to you, professionally and personally?
↪ How do you want to make people feel through your work?
↪ What legacy would you like to leave with your work?
↪ What impact do you wish to have?
↪ Why do you believe you have to do this work? What's calling you?
↪ What's the purpose of your work?

To me, purpose is the single most important part of any business. You need to know your *why*: why you're doing what you're doing, what you're trying to achieve, why you care. It's not just how you do things, but why you're doing them. This is your North Star, your way home: understanding your *why* is key to unlocking true potential for your career.

Of course, your business needs a *why* too. Need some inspiration? Here are a few ideas: the *why* might be:

↪ a problem you're trying to solve;
↪ a social change you want to bring about;
↪ an innovative product or service you want people to experience.

It's good to have a simple and straightforward *why*: this makes it easier to be built into a company vision and communicated to consumers. Business doesn't need to be complicated. Some of the best businesses in the world are those with a simple mission statement. Don't know where to start? Dig deep and ask yourself what kind of change you want to bring about in the world.

For me, the *why* of About Time was believing that time is precious and we're not careful enough with how we spend it. I believe that time is the most important commodity we have. It's the thing that people talk the most about on their death beds and the thing we regret wasting the most. Telling people how to spend their time in a way that matters was a founding belief at the core of the magazine. I was inspired by a Zadie Smith quote from *On Beauty*:

Time is how you spend your love.[2]

Whenever I have a business decision to make, I come back to that *why*. I ask myself, is this really worth people's time? Does this further the message of the business? The answer usually helps guide my decision-making process. Your *why* is your internal compass in business. Having a list of founding beliefs that you can come back to is a great way to stay grounded and focused. Saasha Celestial-One, the Founder of Olio – a food-sharing app that helps tackle the massive problem of food waste in the UK – advised me that sometimes your *why* comes out of knowing what you *don't* want to be, as much as what you do.

Your *why* can be as ambitious as you like – but the key is *you* have to believe in its potential to grow. Perhaps there's a change you'd like to bring about in society or awareness you'd like to bring to an issue.

Not everyone knows what they wish to dedicate their life – and company – to. If you're feeling overwhelmed, the questions below might help guide you towards the *why* in your career and help you uncover some hidden passions.

WORKBOOK

Q1: Do you know your company's why? What's your personal drive?

_____

_____

_____

_____

Q2: What motivates and inspires you to do the work that you're
doing? List three things.

_____

_____

_____

_____

Q3: How can you translate your why into the day-to-day of the
brand? How can you broadcast your message far and wide?

_____

_____

_____

_____

_____

Q4: What brands do you really admire and why? What are their
personal mission statements? How do they translate these
messages well?

_____

_____

_____

_____

_____

Q5: What do you want the company to achieve? In a year and in
five years.

_____

_____

_____

_____

Q6: What markers can you put in place to help measure your
progress towards that vision? List three targets that will
measure the company's success in achieving the 'why'.

_____

_____

_____

_____

CASE STUDY   She Made It: Serena Guen

Name: Serena Guen

Job title: Founder of SUITCASE Magazine and Agency

How did you first come up with the idea for SUITCASE Magazine?

I first came up with the idea of SUITCASE Magazine when I was at university. I had always loved travelling and came from quite a multicultural background, but I was quite surprised by how inaccurate (and often ugly!) travel media was.

I've always been the go-to person for travel recommendations with my friends; I started creating little guides for friends and they'd send them to friends of friends. And then one day, one of my friends said, 'Oh, I've got the best guide to Paris' – it turned out it was the one I had written. This gave me confidence and the concept really grew from there!

For me, the world is so beautiful, and I wanted to create a magazine that is both visually stunning, practical and inspirational. I was very inspired by *National Geographic's* photography and wanted to create something that was the next generation of that – beautiful, collective, but a lot more accessible, cool and practical.

What do you think is the key to SUITCASE's success?

I think the key to our success has to been to work hard and stick to our mission, which was to deliver high-quality content to our audience.

Yes, we could have raised loads of money. We could have scaled really fast. But then we would have lost the essence of who we are. I think many brands forget that and they get swept up in this feeling of 'we need to grow really quickly!', but then many of them don't actually make it through.

In terms of SUITCASE, I wouldn't even say that we're successful yet. There's a lot to do still. But one of the key learnings for me was to understand my strengths and weaknesses – to really continually question and assess them. I ask myself: am I in the best role for my company? Am I doing the right thing?

I've changed roles many times in the business, first as Editor-in-Chief, then CEO and more recently I've just hired a CEO and I've stepped into a new role again as Executive Chairwoman. At different points of the company, I've realized who I need to bring on or empower within the team to make the business as successful as it can be.

There's no point in clinging on to something if it's not what you are best at or what you enjoy, because the rest of the company will suffer for it. Bringing on a new CEO is one the best things I've ever done – it's quite unusual for a founder to do at this stage in the lifecycle.

But I felt like we had hit a wall in terms of how quickly we were growing and could just achieve things much better if we had someone who was more experienced in the travel and media industries. I need someone better in terms of management and scaling businesses – I was pleased to bring on a female CEO because I don't think there are enough of us.

How do you make your brand stand out in a crowded marketplace?

One of the most important things that any brand can do is create a brand book, which they live and die by. That's something we created at the beginning of SUITCASE, but we didn't look at enough during our lifecycle. We've just gone through the process of revamping it now – it really helps us make all decisions more easily.

One way that you can think about your brand is as a person: does your brand personify someone? Is this someone you'd like to hang out with? What do they represent? What do they stand for?

Those questions guide a lot of your brand values. In terms of the product, we make sure that compared with a lot of the travel media companies, we care. That comes across in the quality of the content, the way we research pieces and our settings.

Do you think it's important for young brands to be disruptive?

More than being disruptive, it's important for young brands to cater to their audience really well.

I think there are so many problems yet to be solved. For example, in travel, the average person is going on 30 websites before booking something. That journey is ridiculous and not streamlined at all!

So, I think the best thing you can do as a young person who is starting a business is to really nail down your user persona. Understand exactly what they want and need rather than being disruptive for the sake of it.

Do you think you've been held back as a female founder?

I feel I've been held back as a female founder in two ways. The first is perhaps smaller. I think you have to be a little bit savvier about meeting men, especially older men. Especially when you meet someone that's high-powered from a company that you really want to work with and they suggest a drinks meeting. I didn't used to think a lot of it, but now from my experience I won't do that again. I make it very clear where the boundary is and who I am as a person. Lunch and coffee meetings only now!

However, honestly, the hardest thing for me as a female founder was raising money. You could say it's always difficult to raise money for a travel or media business anyway, but I felt as a female founder, I was constantly in a room with people who didn't look like me.

They were mainly older, which of course there's nothing wrong with, but I couldn't help feeling they didn't 'get' the products because *they* weren't the target audience. So when it came to choosing whether to invest or not, it was more difficult to get them to understand why that product was relevant.

I'm really glad I found some amazing investors in the end, but I think there's a reason why so little investment, especially VC [venture capital] investment, goes into female founders every year. That really needs to change and I'm pleased to see the rise in female VCs and angel investors.

CHAPTER THREE

How to think like an entrepreneur

Mindset is everything. One thing that all the case studies in this book have in common is a positive mindset – an outlook of hope that helps them be resilient in the face of adversity.

We know that mindset is particularly relevant for female founders, as the culture around entrepreneurship is still male-dominant. Studies would show that women are much less likely to think of themselves as CEOs – in the 2019 Rose Review, it was shown that the cumulative effect of women's different decisions along the entrepreneurial journey (the four key stages are: intention to start a business, startup, sustain and scale) is that men in the UK are five times more likely than women to build a business of £1 million+ turnover.[1]

There are so many factors that help determine the success of one business against a competitor. Of course, a good business plan, financial backing and quality concept matter, but mindset and confidence play a huge role. I've seen first-hand businesses that have flourished because of the sheer enthusiasm, resilience and positivity of their founder.

But how can you give yourself the best possible chance at success? What attitude do you need to adopt to make your business thrive? How can you think like a successful female founder?

One of the most important things, I think, is to stay in your lane – don't be put off by what you perceive as other people's success around you. We often see a snapshot of someone's life or career through social media – and subconsciously let those messages chip away at our own self-belief. Positivity and resilience aren't really innate to *any* of us – they're like a muscle you need to learn to flex, and there's some very clear, practical steps you can take to do that.

How to be more positive

There is no doubt that being positive and having an optimistic outlook is going to serve you well in the future. If *you* don't believe in what you're doing, you can't expect others to.

Being positive is a great way to build a great culture – for your customers and your employees. But what if you don't always feel positive? What if your first instinct is to think the worst? It doesn't mean that naturally cautious people shouldn't do business, but I do think you can and *should* work on your positivity mindset to give yourself the best chance at success. Here are my top tips for building a positive mindset:

Stay accountable to your vision

Why do you want to launch your own business? What currently frustrates you about your work? Get clear on the *positives* you think running your own thing will bring for your life. If there are aspects you're not happy with in your current work setup, use these as inspiration to create something better. Positive mindset means not dwelling on what you don't want and, instead, manifesting what you *do* want.

Channel negative experiences into positive desires for your future. For example, rather than wanting to run from your horrible, egomaniac boss, you can reframe it as a desire to create a happy work culture at your own company.

Celebrate your successes

When was the last time you celebrated yourself? It's so easy to glaze over your wins as if they barely happened, but spend ages dwelling on all the things that have gone wrong. We rarely give ourselves the time and space to celebrate the successes and are always ready to beat ourselves up about something that didn't work out. Celebrate your successes! Reward yourself! Celebrate any progress – remember, if you're the boss, there might be no one handing out praise like when you're an employee, so you've got to do it for yourself.

Journal your achievements

It's easy to forget to take stock with your own business. Spending time at the end of every week, writing down all the things that went *right*, is so helpful. This doesn't need to be fancy or intimidating – you can simply pop some thoughts into your phone or a notebook – but it's a great way to keep yourself accountable. Perhaps it's as simple as a good conversation you had, a new client signed or some nice feedback? It will make a world of difference when things go pear-shaped. It serves as a reminder that you are capable of success. People don't fail; plans do. Take a deep breath and come back to things with fresh perspective. Studies show that if you express gratitude, it raises your happiness by 25 per cent, so try to incorporate weekly gratitude journaling into your business life.

Set realistic, smaller goals

Goals can be these big, intangible things we use to track our success – the yardstick to measure our own self-worth. But what are they, really? Just something we've decided for ourselves. The key to feeling successful every day is to give yourself smaller, more realistic goals. It might not mean winning a new job, or getting a new stockist for your product, but it can be something as simple as having an encouraging phone call or coffee with a potential new client.

When it comes to self-employment, there's going to be so many challenges. Things are not going to go to plan, cash is going to be tight at times, there are going to be moments of despair, and the bigger the goal, the more pressure you're putting on yourself. Breaking your goals down into more manageable chunks will help you build a sustainable business that grows at a healthy rate.

WORKBOOK

Q1: How much time do I spend celebrating success? Do I dwell too long on failure? What are three things that I could do when something goes right that would make me feel great?

_____

_____

_____

_____

Q2: How often do I take stock of the things that are going right? Could I be better at writing down my achievements and where could this fit into my week?

_____

_____

_____

_____

Q3: How big are the goals I set myself? Could I make some
actionable goals? List three goals you'd like to achieve this
week and why.

_____

_____

_____

_____

Q4: Do you surround yourself with positive or negative people?
How can you reduce the negativity in your life?

_____

_____

_____

_____

CASE STUDY   She Made It: Camilla Barnard

Name: Camilla Barnard
Job title: Co-founder of Rude Health

How did the idea for Rude Health come about?

It started from a really simple concept. Back in 2006, we felt that
breakfast cereals weren't as good as they could be. In particular,
healthier cereals like muesli were just not that exciting. There was
nothing on shelves that you looked at and thought, 'Oh that looks
delicious.' That was the fundamental belief: that there's no reason why
something nourishing shouldn't also taste good.

We started it at the kitchen table with very little money. We had
£4,000, which we used to buy the tubs, ingredients and some branded
aprons – and we'd take our cereals to local delis. It was just enough to
get us going, and that was all. We survived on what came in for the first
couple of years. We didn't know where it was going to go, and we didn't
have a clear plan.

Our timing was quite good back then. In 2006, premium organic food was growing in popularity. The retailers said they liked it, but it was too expensive – we were making muesli with 26 ingredients. In the end, we got listed with Marigold, got ourselves in Whole Foods and Riverford. It all built from there!

Where's Rude Health now?

Now we're 13 years into running Rude Health – we're looking at international growth, lots of new food and drinks, and business development, which is all very exciting. We've become one of the biggest brands in the UK in our category. When we started years ago, I'd never worked in food before, neither had my husband or the other two people who started the business with us, so we were really getting into something we had absolutely no idea about – which is probably why we did it. The less you know, the less you fear!

Do you have any advice on creating an exciting brand look and voice?

A brand is a personality. It really helps to look at it like that. When you're coming up with a brief, you're effectively describing a person. When you can do that clearly, it's going to be much easier for an agency to bring it to life. Work out who you are as a brand, your values, beliefs and what you stand for. It's easier for a designer to convert that into a visual.

Before launching, did you see yourself an as entrepreneurial person?

I'd always had a hankering to start my own business. When I was at university, someone asked me what I wanted to do and I said own a vineyard. No one in my family has their own business so I don't know where it came from. I think it's an independent streak more than a particularly entrepreneurial streak. I don't want to do what someone else says. I see 'entrepreneurial' as someone who keeps starting businesses, but I don't think that's me.

What kind of mindset do you think you need to run a business of your own?

I've learned that there's no one, single way to be in business. For me, I couldn't have run a business on my own – I absolutely needed a partner to do it with, although that's not the same for everybody. It's a common problem, though, it's really hard on your own. You need someone to let off steam with, someone who's up when you're down, balance your skills with, celebrate with. Another thing is your business is 24 hours a day, 365 days a year and a real full-time job. You have to be committed. You've got to learn to stick at it. It's taken 13 years of hard work for Rude Health to become what it is. Nothing was overnight for us.

How do you stick at it when it's really hard work?

Running your own business is constant learning and finding parts that you really love (for me that's making the new food and drinks). Learning, commitment, being prepared for a bit of a slog – I might have run away if I knew how hard it was going to be!

What makes you believe in yourself as an entrepreneur?

I didn't always believe in myself. I thought business was what other, more sparkly people did. But this business hasn't happened by accident – I was there, I was part of it, I made it happen. I can now give myself that credit. Being self-doubting is a better way to be as a businessperson than overly confident, because it means you're willing to learn and listen to people. It has some advantages, doubting yourself.

How to be more resilient

Resilience is something often discussed at our events; I love hearing female entrepreneurs sharing their stories about how they bounce back from knocks, disappointments and failures. Resilience is one of the most important qualities you need to succeed in business – but where does it come from? What *is* resilience and how do we build it up? Here are a few things I've learned about being resilient:

Work on yourself first

Resilience is about inner confidence, knowing yourself, your mind and having strength in your convictions. If you're going into business full of self-doubt, you're already starting at a disadvantage. You have to work on yourself, outside of the office or boardroom, before you can launch into something that's going to be full of challenges. Take the time to build up your self-confidence – this might mean surrounding yourself with positive people, doing physical exercise that makes you feel great or working with a careers coach. The difference between a success-ful business and one that goes to startup heaven can be the emotional resilience of the founder leading it. So: build yourself up, find a place of self-confidence and create the career you dream of.

Imagine the worst

No, really. Imagine it. Visualize it. Get comfortable with it. What if the worst-case scenario is realized, what do you do? How do you feel? So often with About Time, I have feared the worst – that our cash flow was all wrong, that I would have to let staff go, that the magazine was attacked by a cyber bug. Allowing myself to have those fears, listen to them and imagine what would happen if they were real takes the sting out.

In fact, pushing those thoughts to the back of your mind is the worst thing you can do. They never really go away, just linger and make you uneasy. Give yourself the space to confront those fears head on and visualize what your response and action would be if they came true. You'll build up your resilience to problems simply by having a plan of action. Find a place where your thoughts can run free – whether it's a walk in the park, whilst driving or going for a swim – and face your fears.

Surround yourself with great people

We all have friends who are willing to sit in the pub with us for hours, talking our problems to death, but sometimes what you need is a friend who will give you *practical* advice. Running a business is like a romantic relationship. There will be early-days problems, miscommunication, lots of false starts and you'll want to walk away at some point. You need a practical, switched-on friend you can talk to openly about these things. If you don't have this person, go out and find them at networking events in your industry – you can look on Eventbrite for great panel talks or networking breakfasts. Look for someone who can be your practical friend, who you can always call for advice.

WORKBOOK

Q1: How confident do I feel about my business and about myself?

_____

_____

_____

Q2: What can I do to build my confidence – what makes me feel great?

_____

_____

_____

Q3: What's the worst that can happen? What am I scared of? Take time to visualize the worst-case scenario for you and your business.

_____

_____

_____

_____

Q4: Who do I wish to surround myself with? Who can I confide in
to help support me?

_____

_____

_____

How to stop comparing yourself with others

Comparison is an absolute killer with business. By comparing ourselves with others and their successes, we can lose sight of ourselves, our goals and our business.

It's not easy to stop yourself comparing. Thanks to social media, we can know exactly what other people's days, careers, holidays, romances and successes look like. Comparison is obviously not healthy, and one of the most detrimental things for aspiring entrepreneurs is comparing yourself and your success with others. How can you stop that relentless loop of comparison and self-criticism?

I've been in digital media for five years and I've seen a lot of businesses of the same kind launch in my time. So often, someone has rung me up telling me about a new magazine which is 'exactly like yours', and now I just take a deep breath, smile and laugh it off. I no longer fight the urge to feel threatened. I have learned in my time in the industry that competitors will always come and go. Allowing yourself to feel threatened by a business that's similar to yours is wasted emotion; it provides you with nothing, just an extra helping of self-doubt. Here's what I've learned about comparison and how to combat it:

Question why you're feeling threatened

It's important to ask yourself why you're feeling threatened by competition. Are you resting on your laurels? Have you been doing something that's easy to replicate? Do you realize you're not adding unique value to your industry? Dig deep and ask yourself some tough questions about your business and offering. You might find that you're feeling threatened because your business has lost its USP (unique selling point) or your message has lost its impact. This might be a trip back to the drawing board to remind yourself why your business is different, set some new goals or create a fresh marketing strategy.

Use competition as motivation

The term 'healthy competition' exists for a reason. It can be a great motivator for you and your business. Rather than feeling threatened when something similar to your business launches, see it as a validation for proof of concept. You're obviously on to something if there are copy-cat companies! Rather than feeling disheartened by a new competitor, ask yourself: what can we do better? How can we add value to our brand or offering? What makes us special? Sometimes the presence of a new competitor can force you into thinking once again about your offering and how you communicate your brand message. If you make yourself see competition as a positive force, one that makes you sit up and think 'hell, this is going to make us work even harder,' you've turned a negative situation into a positive one.

Curb what you consume

Oh boy, is this one important. The unceasing scrolling on Instagram, the bombardment of information on your Twitter timelines, the promotion updates on LinkedIn, it all contributes to our feeling of self-worth. Let me say it once again: *curate* your online world. Decide carefully who you follow, and measure how their social media presence makes you feel about yourself and your work. You owe more to your mental health than you do to other people's follower numbers on Instagram.

Social media needs to be used mindfully; although it provides opportunities for you and your brand, it also opens up a huge amount of never-before-seen information about other people's worlds. If you find yourself falling into a trap of endless scrolling and comparison, I would start to take note of how you feel after spending time on different social media platforms. Do you feel discouraged after seeing photos on Instagram? Does Twitter make you feel worse about your company's success? First, try curating your feed more – unfollow the accounts that make you feel bad, mute keywords, tune out from the noise that's affecting how you feel about your own journey.

Remember to switch off

For me, running an online business means spending hundreds of hours online every week and it's become vital to step away from social media on a regular basis. I find that logging out of all my social media accounts on a Friday night after work and not logging in again until Monday morning does wonders for my mental health. If your business relies on social media over the weekend, schedule your posts in advance – I use Buffer for this and you can still measure your reach using Bit.ly. We're so accustomed to having social media in our everyday lives that we've forgotten what life was like before it. Constantly comparing your work with others is wasted energy. Step away. You'll feel a million times better.

WORKBOOK

Q1: Why are you feeling threatened by a new competitor? Is there something deeper within that?

_____

_____

_____

_____

Q2: What is the USP of your brand and offering? What makes you different from other companies or individuals?

_____
_____
_____
_____

Q3: Are there certain social media accounts or platforms that make you feel bad? Who could you unfollow that might be good for your mental health?

_____
_____
_____
_____

Q4: When can you take a social media detox? How realistic is it for you to step away from social media once a week, and if not, why not? Can you find a solution around this?

_____
_____
_____
_____

CASE STUDY   She Made It: Kat Horrocks

Name: Kat Horrocks

Job title: Women's life and career coach

How did you get into the work you're doing now?

Before coaching, I was a bridal make-up artist and ran my own freelance business in that industry for four years. I craved more flexibility and wanted a career change to something that felt sustainable for me long term. Coaching was a great fit because I love the one-to-one connection I can create with women, and going deeper with their goals, career, confidence and personal development.

How did you find higher purpose with your work?

I personally connect with my purpose through doing! You must allow yourself to be a beginner and be willing to try something new, even when it's scary. We hope that purpose is something we 'arrive' at one day, but, in fact, it's more like a puzzle that pieces together over time. *'Clarity comes from action, not thought'* really resonates with me – we need to begin simply by *doing*.

How do you measure success for yourself?

Success is incredibly personal – don't measure yourself by anyone else's definition but your own. Challenge what society views as success and ask yourself: what really makes me happy?

Success for one woman could be having the flexibility to pick her kids up a few days a week. Success for another woman could be being able to work from anywhere and travel the world. And success for another woman could simply mean being able to pay her bills so she can enjoy herself and not stress. It's trusting and being okay with how you define success, whatever that may look like to you.

How important is mindset when it comes to success?

Mindset is everything! Often, we know what we want and how to get it – we know exactly what we'd say to a friend in the same situation. And yet we're unable to give ourselves that support. There are often invisible obstacles in the way of taking action – imposter syndrome, confidence, perfectionism or other hurdles – which need to be overcome in order to move forward.

QUICK TIPS: GETTING INTO A SUCCESS MINDSET

↳ Keep an evidence bank. This is a place where you collate all the awesome things about you. List all your positive previous experiences, successes and accolades. Whenever something new comes in – positive feedback via email or even a personal win that you've challenged yourself to do – write it down. Next time that critical voice crops up telling you you're not good enough, head back to this bank of evidence.

↳ Acting as if. There's a myth that once the success comes, the confidence or positive attitude will arrive. In reality, we must be brave and put ourselves out there in order to be in the right place at the right time. A question I love clients to ask themselves is, 'what would the bravest version of me do today?' This is a challenge to get you out of your comfort zone and continue to push forward with your goals.

How important is goal-setting?

What gets measured gets managed. I recommend everyone has a regular check-in point with their life and career goals and asks themselves:

↳ What's my progress like?
↳ Do my goals still inspire me?
↳ How can I improve and where do I go from here?
↳ What do I need to focus on in the coming weeks and months?

When it comes to achieving goals, you have to put yourself first. It's so easy to let the day-to-day tasks swamp your schedule; with long-term goals, you have to actively prioritize them – whether that means doing them first or setting aside dedicated time in your calendar (for example, no meetings on Fridays to prioritize business growth). If you have to wait to have free time to work on your goals, you'll be waiting forever!

CHAPTER FOUR

How to define what success means to you

When I say success, what do you think of? Perhaps your interpretation of success is financial, such as buying a house, moving abroad or providing for your family. Perhaps success to you is emotional, such as *feeling* a sense of security, being fulfilled by your work or reaching goals. I hope it's a mixture of the two – loving what you do, plus reaping financial rewards from it.

The truth is, there's no one definition of success. As a society, we've come to attach a huge amount of meaning to the tangible, material signs of success, like getting on the property ladder, wearing head-to-toe Lulu Lemon or driving a nice car, but even people who have achieved these things in plenty *still* don't feel successful. Why? Because success is a feeling, not a destination.

It's the case that we're often still riddled with self-doubt, comparison and imposter syndrome, even *when* we've achieved some of the things that society deems a marker of success. This is especially true of women, who find it hard to own their success, and will attribute it to chance.

The amount of times I've complimented a woman on how well she's doing, only for her to bat it off by saying, 'Oh, I just got lucky,' or, 'It's not really like it seems.' Success is a funny thing; something we try so hard to achieve, only to shy away from owning it the second we're in touching distance.

Why do we struggle to feel successful? Perhaps we overlook the individual nature of success – the fact that for everyone, it will look and feel different, and unless you are clear on your own version of success, you'll be constantly comparing yourself with others. And, of course, if you're always comparing your success with others, you'll never feel fully happy. Success, particularly for women, is a process of staying open and curious. Success is not a destination. Discover what matters to you in life – identify the goals, rewards and milestones for your personal journey.

In this chapter, we're going to dip deep into your personal definition of success. I want you to get into the habit of seeing success as fluid and flexible. Treat your work life with playful curiosity – our goals, mission and purpose are ever-changing, and, most likely, our definition of success will shift over time. For example, when I was 22, success in my business looked like glamorous invites, new experiences and travelling the world, whereas success at 29 looks like being able to shut my laptop at 6pm, not working weekends and having a sense of financial wellbeing that calms my mind.

Checking in with myself on a regular basis, creating space in my week to reflect, question and plan, has given me clarity on those ever-shifting goals. You must be especially curious with *yourself* – for me, staying true to my own definition of success has come from continually asking myself questions about my business and life. Am I enjoying this? Does my work fulfil me right now? Is my business supporting my life goals right now? Interviewing yourself from time to time will help you feel more connected and aligned with your work.

Remember to be kind and gentle with yourself. It's okay if you realize you're very far from the things that will make you feel aligned and driven. Success in business is a constantly evolving process – and you may need time to work out what that looks like to you. The important thing is that you identify them – that's the first step. And then we can work on the practical steps to making those goals a reality!

Now let's work out your personal definition of success.

EXERCISE: UNDERSTANDING WHAT SUCCESS MEANS TO YOU

Imagine, for a moment, that you're in a job interview. The twist is that you're interviewing yourself. Try to be as honest and true to yourself as you answer the below with a pen and paper:

1 When I say success, what do you think of? Or who? Write down any associations you have with success and any people who spring to mind.

2 Why, do you think, do you associate those things with success?

3 If your career could provide three things to you right now, what would they be and why?

4 Some of the financial goals I want to achieve with my career are...

5 Some of the emotional goals I want to achieve with my career are...

6 I will feel successful, when...

7 Where have I already seen success in my life?

8 How can I continue to build on that success?

9 What is my biggest achievement at work? What am I most proud of?

10 What have I learned about myself from previous successes?

It's important to understand the associations you personally have with success. This might be a role model that you really look up to, or it might be a certain lifestyle. For example, for me, part of my definition of success is being able to work anywhere in the world. The freedom and ability to travel whilst working is more important to me, emotionally, than any number in my bank balance.

It's a good idea to unpick some of your associations with success. Why is it, do you think, that these things will make you feel successful and fulfilled? Are they things you truly want? Or has someone told you that these things are important – a parent, perhaps, who's encouraged you to pursue a particular route, or a friend, perhaps, who's laughed at your true desires and said they are 'unrealistic'? I think we should all have an element of the unrealistic to make life exciting. Being realistic often means playing safe. The more unrealistic our goals, the bigger we're dreaming – that's no bad thing.

Why do you want to start your own business? Identifying the three things that your new career can provide to you gives you focus and clarity. Perhaps those three things are freedom, flexibility and autonomy, so you can focus on your career whilst picking up your kids from the school gates. Remember, there's no wrong or right answer, there's only what feels authentic to you.

Now, on financial goals, I don't think we should set financial goals alone for our work – it's not enough to drive you, and especially when it's your own business; you need passion and motivation too. But, of course, they are important – you have to eat, have a roof over your head and feel a sense of momentum in your business. What I've learned, from interviewing hundreds of entrepreneurs, is that financial goals are actually, in the deeper sense, connected to a sense of wellbeing and abundance.

It's not that we necessarily want more money; we just want to feel calmer and more relaxed with money. We want to feel that money flows towards us, and, when needed, we're able to earn more. Financial wellbeing is, of course, linked to our emotional wellbeing – it's hard to feel calm when you're constantly stressed about money, so understanding how finance fits into your definition of success is important.

Isolate the financial goals you want to achieve with your business – this could be having a certain amount of reserve in the bank, business turnover or paying into a private pension – and then look at your emotional goals. You might be surprised how linked they are; you might find that one of your financial goals is to manage your cash flow better, and one of your emotional goals is to feel less stressed towards the end of the month. They are, of course, part of the same story. Success as an entrepreneur is also about understanding yourself as a whole, and the connection between your work and your emotional wellbeing.

By answering *I will feel successful when...*, you may surprise yourself. Again, it could be a feeling. Perhaps it's, *I will feel successful when I stop doubting myself.* Or, it might be something singular and tangible, *I will feel successful when I've done a TEDx Talk.* I would suggest that you make this one goal really clear to yourself – and something ongoing, such as self-confidence. Keep it as something you can constantly come back to. Focus your energy on it, and you'll be working towards it, even when you don't realize it. We manifest things for ourselves when we're honest that we want them, after all.

In the early stages of launching something new, you may feel self-doubt. This is normal – you may be doing something new to you, often with little experience, and you're having to pick up lots of new skills along the way. You're not going to get everything right, but remembering where you've felt successful or achieved things in the past can be a good source of self-confidence. Recall where you've already seen success before – what happened, what did it look and feel like? Perhaps there was a particular achievement you're proud of, or something big that you overcame. Draw on previous successes to give you strength and motivation now. And how can you build on that now? It might be a case of a new skill you picked up previously, such as public speaking, that you may want to build upon now.

And, finally, question what you've learned about yourself from previous successes. It might be that you're more capable than you think. It might be that you're able to lead a team or do that big presentation. We tend to assume that our thoughts about ourselves are true, especially the negative ones, such as we're not able to do something, but looking back on where you've proved yourself wrong is a good way to disassociate with these negative self-beliefs. You're more capable, strong and powerful than you realize. Allow yourself to believe that.

TOP TIPS: INTERNALIZING YOUR SUCCESS

Here are a few tips that I've picked up whilst running my business that have helped me *feel* success more. If you want to reduce self-doubt and boost your confidence, try these top tips:

↳ **Write down goals.** You can't measure your progress, unless you have something to measure against. You might feel cringed out or embarrassed by this, but it's healthy to set targets for your business. I like to do a monthly review of my goals – treat yourself as an employee of your company and take your progress seriously.

↳ **Cultivate a growth mindset.** I think it's important to reframe rejection. I only allow myself a limited amount of time to feel down or dejected when something doesn't happen for me or my business, and then I force myself to move on. A growth mindset means you see everything as an opportunity to grow.

↳ **See obstacles as opportunities.** You cannot fear obstacles in business – they are literally everywhere. At times, every way you turn, things are going to seem hard. Obstacles are for a reason – to challenge and push us. The important thing is not to internalize either obstacles or rejection as personal failing. People don't fail. Plans and strategy fail – you probably just need a new plan. Sit down and literally imagine this obstacle in the middle of the road: what do you need to get around it?

↳ **Get into nature.** Office environments can make us feel constrained, hemmed in and stressed. We're not designed to be at a desk for hours at a time, surrounded by four walls. These environments can multiply our stress and make us feel lacking in creativity. Getting out into nature allows us fresh perspective on situations and allows our minds space to wander. Try to go for a nature walk every day and switch your phone into airplane mode.

↳ **Keep a success and gratitude journal.** Take time every week to track your success and positives of the week – gratitude does wonders for your mindset.

↳ **Invest in yourself.** When you're feeling run down and overtired, you're never going to be the best version of yourself. Investing in yourself might be different for everyone – whether it's investing in a mentor, coach, workshop or an act of self-care. Make yourself a priority in your business.

Become a goal-getter

A helpful way of building your business is by creating clear short-term and long-term goals. Short-term goals are things that can be achieved over the next three to six months, whereas your long-term goals might take up to 12 months.

Create a monthly review to measure your progress – looking at the practical steps you need to keep moving with these goals. Remember: everything needs to be broken down into manageable actions, otherwise you won't carve out necessary time or energy to make stuff happen. Here's a guide to how you create a goal-tracker – I'm a paper person and love writing by hand, but you may want to create a digital template like below.

GOAL-GETTER: SHORT-TERM GOALS

My goal:

How will I feel achieving this goal?

How long will it take to achieve this goal?

Things to do to achieve this goal – list five things:

Key milestones to track this goal – list three things:

Goal completion date:

GOAL-GETTER: LONG-TERM GOALS

My goal:

How will I feel achieving this goal?

How long will it take to achieve this goal?

Why is this goal important to me?

Things to do to achieve this goal – list 10 things:

Key milestones to track this goal – list three things:

Goal completion date:

The process of discovering what motivates and drives you, and the steps needed to make magic happen, takes time and energy. It involves investment in yourself – to actually sit with yourself and listen. That's what it means to be an entrepreneur – to listen to your soul's desires and make them real. Take the time. Listen, learn, be curious.

WORKBOOK

Q1: What have you learned about success from this chapter?

_____

_____

_____

_____

Q2: What do you want to change about how you see success?

_____

_____

_____

_____

Q3: How much does success matter to you and what does it now look like?

_____

_____

_____

_____

Q4: What do you want to change about how you see success from now on?

_____

_____

_____

_____

CASE STUDY   She Made It: Ruth Kudzi

Name: Ruth Kudzi
Job title: Mindset coach, coach trainer, best-selling author

How did you end up doing the work you're doing now?

I had always been interested in coaching since doing my first degree in Management and Psychology. Over the years I had been coached by managers and in 2010 I got accepted on a fast-track leadership programme where I got my own coach. As soon as we started having coaching sessions, the penny dropped: this was what I wanted to do. I started to blend coaching into my leadership approach and then did some voluntary work as a coach before training and starting my own business four years ago.

What does success mean to you?

Success means impact; helping others create businesses that work for them and giving me sufficient income that I have choices for me and my family.

What do you think holds women back when it comes to reaching their true potential?

Conflicting demands: the fact that they feel that they need to do and be everything. A lack of role models is another factor as there are still more men who are in the higher levels of business. A lack of confidence and self-belief comes into it as well. Many women don't think they are good enough and feel they need to be different or better to succeed.

How does our relationship with success change over time?

I think it becomes more internal – what motivates us intrinsically rather than the external measures.

How can we stop comparing ourselves with others?

By dialling down on what you are here to do and focusing on accomplishment rather than performance-based goals, we can then measure our success in terms of growth rather than a more pass or fail measure. By stepping into and owning everything about yourself – your shadows as well as the light – you are able to stop the comparison and do as the Instagram memes say: step into your lane.

What are your top five tips for getting into a 'success mindset'?

- Focus on gratitude and what you have achieved.
- Ask yourself what you have learned rather than what you have achieved.
- Surround yourself with people who are positive and optimistic.

- Ask for help from others who are in front of you.

- Be a badass with your boundaries.

Are there any exercises you love to help work on mindset and success?

- Practise gratitude every single day by writing down three things that you are grateful for.

- When you are making decisions, take some time to tune into what your gut is telling you and then ask yourself if there is anything else you need to attend to.

- Measure your progress and always focus on what you can learn and where you can grow.

CHAPTER FIVE

How to maximize your skill set

Remember what life was like before the world told you what you *should* be doing? Before you stopped pursuing your interests? Before people told you that your dreams were too big, too risky, too unrealistic? Before you forgot to do things just for the joy of it?

What makes you happy at work? Most of the time, the things that make us the happiest are those that we do best in. We excel at things we think we're good at. We get better at them because we're excelling. It's a circle of self-belief, confidence and fulfilment, which is the secret to making our productivity soar.

Want to be more productive? Focus on the fulfilment factor.

Feel you're not doing well at something? It's probably because you're not really enjoying the task at hand.

You're not being productive. You're dragging your heels. You find yourself browsing through Facebook rather than doing it. You're out of alignment with your purpose and, hence, your productivity, because your heart isn't really into it. You're meant to enjoy your work. Don't let anyone convince you otherwise.

Think back to childhood – what were the things you loved at school? The sports and subjects you enjoyed, you always did best in? Hated maths? You probably didn't do well in it. Loved English? You probably thought you were good at it. The things you gleaned the most pleasure out of, you thrived in. Naturally, it feels good to excel in your work.

Our passions drive our productivity. Nothing really changes as we get older, other than we lose sight of the things we love. We're thrust into the working world and told that work should feel, well, hard. It's meant to be a slog, because serious graft is the price you pay for success, right? We're not meant to really *enjoy* our work, right?

We can easily fall into soulless career paths – for the sake of stability or because our parents want us to – and we forget to *enjoy* what we do. We lose sight of the fact that fun and pleasure are paramount to having a fulfilling career. And then we find ourselves, at 45, in a career we hate and having to take a radical sabbatical and become a yoga teacher in Bali. There's absolutely nothing wrong with that, of course, but wouldn't it be nice if you didn't *have* to have a 'sudden wake-up call' and find yourself starting all over again professionally? Wouldn't it be nice to love your work, from the start?

For me, part of the joy of self-employment is taking back ownership over the things that bring you joy and creating a career which you both love *and* thrive in. Let's bring back the enjoyment factor into work – forget the notion that hard work needs to feel hard. What if there's another way? Well, there is. A way that nourishes you, not depletes you. A working day that leaves you energized, not drained. Let's discover it together.

EXERCISE: MEET YOUR INNER CHILD

It's time to interview yourself again. Take a moment with a pen and paper to answer these questions honestly:

1 Think back to childhood. What job did you want to do as a child?

2 As a child, what activities did you find most enjoyable?

3 How can you incorporate those into your work life today?

4 What one thing, professionally, excites and terrifies you in equal measure?

5 If you knew there was no chance of failure, what job would you do and why?

6 What practical steps do you need to take to make that dream a reality? List three to five.

7 Visualize a day in the life of your dream career. What does it look like? How do you see yourself? What tasks are you doing?

Now, I know what you're thinking: what does it matter what job I wanted to do as a child? What relevance does that have to my world today? A lot, actually. Our childhood selves are our purest selves – the ones who believed in themselves wholeheartedly, and dared themselves to dream, vision, play. Children don't let the world tell them that they can't do something – they can be astronauts, professional ballet dancers, pop stars, without a hint of self-doubt. The world really starts to open up when you believe in yourself.

But as we get older, we become more afraid. We're scared to take risks. We don't want to jump into the unknown. We don't back ourselves to try something new. We become so fearful of failure that we're too scared to even try. It's no way to live. Pushing through fear, ultimately, is the only choice we have if we want to live our lives to the fullest. It's how we grow.

The things you loved doing as a child – whether it's art, dancing, creative writing – might be something that you can weave into your work life today. Sure, it might not be writing fairy tales all day, but you might find your creativity and love of language expressed through being a creative copywriter for brands, for example. Creative outlets in business are really important; finding ways to express imagination and weave inspiration into your work will help keep it lively and exciting.

It's easy to think that if something scares us, we shouldn't do it. But actually, we *need* to step out of our comfort zone. Fear isn't warning you against something – in fact, it can often be a sign that we're ready to step up and grow.

So, what excites and terrifies you in equal measure? For lots of people, public speaking is terrifying. It's easy in a corporate environment to hide from the spotlight, but when you're an entrepreneur, you need to get comfortable with speaking in public about yourself and your business. It's a great way to do your own PR and build your authority. Get honest with yourself on the things that really scare you with your work – and make a commitment to yourself to feel the fear and do it anyway.

What's stopping you from pursuing the career of your dreams? Moreover, if failure wasn't an option, what would you do? There are plenty of things that I've turned down in the course of my career because the fear of not doing well at them was enough to stop me in my tracks. We can't let our fear create missed opportunities.

Get practical on the steps you need to take to pursue that dream career. Perhaps that might mean taking a course on the evenings or weekends, seeking advice from an industry expert or building up contacts whilst in your current job. Talking to people is a great place to start; even just getting an understanding of the industry you're interested in will help you scope it out. The first step is often the simplest: getting curious.

When I asked you to visualize a day in the life of your dream career, that's the person you're working towards becoming. That vision – of your future self – is going to be stronger than any financial goal, because it's about the *feeling* your work gives you. I want you to remember that no one is a natural-born CEO. Business leaders are made, not born, through hard work and self-belief. Many people grow into their businesses and it's only *on* the job that they pick up the skills needed to run them. Remember, it's never too late to chase a vision – you can do a total career change at any age or stage in life.

There's a new power in doing things just for the joy of it – let's see if we can find a few things that spark joy in you.

EXERCISE: JUST FOR THE JOY OF IT

1 What activities spark joy in you? Name three things.

2 What creative outlets do you enjoy the most? For example, writing, singing, painting.

3 What would weaving more joy into your work life look like for you?

4 What's one new thing you'd love to try at work?

5 What would you do, even if you weren't paid to do it?

Why is doing things just for the joy of it important? Running your own business can be stressful – if you're going to take on that additional pressure, you need to make sure you create space to enjoy it. It's important to have a healthy dose of joy in your work life, otherwise you'll find yourself burnt out in a few years' time, wondering what it's all for.

Whilst we all know it's important to pursue hobbies that spark joy in us in our free time, many of us overlook finding joy in our working day too. After a few years of running About Time solely as a content platform, I found myself craving more human interaction and connection. I was sick of being stuck behind a laptop all day and wanted to interact with our readers. Which is why we launched events, festivals and podcasts, as a way of interacting with our audience more. Getting face-to-face with our readers in a live capacity and speaking on stage sparks serious joy in me – and reminds me of the buzz I used to get as a child taking part in school talent shows.

Something beautiful happens when you allow your work to reconnect you to long-forgotten hobbies and helps create a path of joy for you. One great way of understanding what this might be for you is asking yourself what part of your work right now you would do for free. When you take money out of the equation, what's left behind? Make that thing clear in your mind and focus your energy on doing more of it.

Understanding your skill set

Let's talk skills. Having a sense of your unique skill set is really important when it comes to starting your own business. Understanding your personal strengths and weaknesses will help you shape the kind of business you should be running.

Of course, you can pick up skills along the way – and there are basic skills like digital marketing, accounting and graphic design that are useful no matter what kind of company you run – but having a natural-born interest in something is always useful.

Moreover, understanding your skill set will help with smart hiring, by helping you hire people that complement your own skills. Think of this as your work DNA – it's worth investing time in understanding your personal strengths and weaknesses, and then you can build outwards from there. The best hires are ones that plug in the gaps of your knowledge – that's what helps your business grow.

Interestingly, I've found a lot of people have a certain close proximity blindness to their own skill set – they are unable to correctly identify their own skills, and often think they're 'bad' at something. Often this self-criticism is historical, as someone once told them so and they took it as fact.

Women, in particular, have a tendency to underplay certain skills and feel they shouldn't pursue something until they are totally ready (whereas men are more likely to jump in at the deep end and learn on the job!). I recommend getting someone else to do the below exercise about you – it might throw up some interesting and unexpected answers!

EXERCISE: UNDERSTANDING YOUR SKILL SET

Take a moment to answer the questions below. If you can get a colleague to answer them about you, that would be great too.

1 What do you identify as your biggest strengths professionally?

2 What are your weak points?

3 What would other people say are your biggest strengths? If in doubt, ask a few friends or colleagues.

4 What skills do you think you need to build on?

5 What practical steps do you need to take to develop these skills? For example, any courses/workshops?

6 How would you rate your leadership skills? Is leadership necessary for you right now?

7 What kind of leader would you like to be? Describe your personal leadership style.

8 List five things that give you the most satisfaction at work.

9 List five things that you don't enjoy at all at work.

The most important thing to remember is that skill sets can and do change – and most skills can be learned along the way.

People skills, for example, is totally something you can learn by exposure – put yourself into situations where you have to interact with people regularly, such as in a customer-facing role, and you'll find that your people skills automatically develop. The problem is that we naturally shy away from things that make us uncomfortable – nobody wakes up saying, 'Today I want to work on my weaknesses,' so we often don't even try. Next time you find yourself in a situation where you feel your natural skill set is being tested, I want you to hold on to that moment. That's something you need to work on and perhaps build up your confidence in – which is a great life learning!

TOP TIPS: BUILDING YOUR SKILL SET

Want to build your skill set? Here are my top tips:

↪ **Identify your weaknesses.** The above exercise will help you with that; alternatively, try to keep a journal of times that you've felt 'out of depth' with your work. Use this as a guide for the areas you need to work on.

↪ **Take a practical course to develop skills.** For some practical skills, such as Photoshop, InDesign or QuickBooks, CityLit in London does some great, affordable short courses. The Open University also offers a wide selection of online courses.

↪ **Skill-swap with another professional.** If you're short on cash, offering your services for free in exchange for learning a skill from another is a great, sociable way to learn.

↪ **Teach yourself on YouTube!** There's so much free information out there now – I taught myself Photoshop through YouTube tutorials.

↪ **Hire a business coach.** Often our weaknesses are not weaknesses at all, but places that we lack confidence. Consider seeing a coach to boost your confidence and try to identify the areas where your own negative self-talk is blocking you.

↪ **Create an informal co-working group.** One way that I've really boosted my work confidence and learned from others is by bringing together a group of self-employed women every month to work together. It's a great way to swap ideas, skills and give each other a morale boost!

Don't be discouraged if you've discovered holes in your skill set through this chapter – #SheMadeIt is here to give you and your business the best possible chance at success, with the tools needed for your work life to flourish.

WORKBOOK

Q1: How would you define your skill set? What are you best at?

_____

_____

_____

_____

Q2: How would other people describe you? What are you often
called at work?

_____

_____

_____

_____

Q3: What are your three biggest skills?

_____

_____

_____

_____

Q4: What skills would you most like to use at work?

_____

_____

_____

_____

Q5: What are your weakest areas at work?

_____

_____

_____

_____

Q6: What three skills would you like to develop the most?

_____

_____

_____

_____

CHAPTER SIX

How to boost your productivity

Feel like you need a productivity lift? This chapter is going to explore all the ways to supercharge your productivity. Being your own boss means managing your time and being accountable for what gets done in a day. Your time is money. Time is also energy, and you want to make sure that you're spending your energy in the best way possible.

Productivity has become one of the buzz words of the 21st century. We're obsessed with it; the concept of getting the most out of our time, milking every minute for all it's worth, and using tools to become a superhuman version of ourselves. Scan the internet and you'll see masses of TEDx Talks on how to boost your productivity by 'hacking' your day – the '5am CEO', micro-dosing on stimulant drugs, breaking up your day with HIIT classes, cold water therapy – it seems that the more extreme, the better.

Honestly, I think we've become obsessed with the idea that there might be some 'secret' to totally hacking our productivity. Hint: there isn't.

What I've learned in the years of running my business is simple: productivity is personal. There is, sadly, no plan, routine or formula that will work for everyone. Productivity begins by understanding your personal work DNA – and how to create a structure and environment that nourishes you.

In this chapter, we're going to unpick the working habits that work best for you and create a structure that you can stick to – one that really works. There's no point creating a routine that leaves you depleted on week one, and then you give up on. Routines are really important; the simple things like waking up at the same time every day, incorporating movement into your day and breaking your day up into manageable tasks really does help. Create a system of working that works for you, for life.

The most important thing I've learned about productivity is that it's best friends with planning. Planning and productivity go hand-in-hand – if you want to get ahead with your work and really measure your progress, you're going to have to learn to plan, plan, plan.

TOP TIPS: HOW TO PLAN YOUR WEEK

1 **Plan the week ahead on a Sunday.** Every Sunday, I take an hour to plan the next week. I fill my diary, book in gym classes, look at where the big work commitments are and try to make sure there's the right balance of down time, so I'm not burnt out by the end of the week. As I'm office-free, I'll look at ways to streamline my week so I'm not wasting unnecessary time on travel.

2 **Plan the day ahead, the night before.** Waking up and feeling the day ahead of you stretch out can be a tad overwhelming when you're self-employed. A simple way to get on top of your working day is to plan your time out the day before, jotting out the particular focus for the morning and afternoon.

3 **Break up your day into manageable chunks.** Be realistic about your schedule. Don't overwhelm yourself with trying to cram in too much into one day. Break your day into smaller chunks – I like to plan my time in 40-minute slots, but you'll have a better sense of how long things take you.

---

4 **Have a focus for the day.** If you run multiple businesses or projects, try to keep a focus for the day. I stick to one theme for the day – I'll tend to only work on one project in a given day.

5 **Book in some fun.** I personally love colour-coordinating my diary, as it's a great way to have a visual representation of the week ahead. In my diary, I use purple for work commitments, green for social occasions and pink for exercise classes. If there's too much purple in my week, then I know I need to book in a bit of fun too!

6 **Factor in down time.** It's really easy to think you need to be go, go, go when you're self-employed. The pressure to network is always there and saying no to work commitments can be hard. But giving yourself time off is, actually, time on, because you'll be a more refreshed, happy version of yourself. Commit to your down time and give yourself permission to relax.

7 **Block out time for admin.** In the early days of my business, staying on top of accounts was a constant battle. I'd let receipts, bills and expenses pile up all month and then feel a huge sense of overwhelm and dread when it came to reconciling my accounts. I now block out the same time every week for these tasks. I find Friday afternoons work best for me, as emails tend to be a little quieter and it means I go into the weekend feeling organized and lighter. Each business is different, but I find two hours is plenty for me to get on top of my finance admin.

8 **Batch together similar tasks.** Batch working is particularly useful if you're doing lots of the same tasks again and again throughout the week – as in the above example, I was spending ages paying invoices, for example, having to log on to my online banking multiple times throughout a day. Keep an eye on the things you find yourself doing repetitively throughout the week and see if you can batch them together.

You can't plan your week properly if you don't know how long things are actually going to take you. Get into the habit, perhaps for a few days, of timing yourself doing certain tasks. Lots of us are chrono-optimistic, thinking tasks take less time than they actually do. By getting a sense of how long tasks actually take you to do, you'll be able to plan your time more wisely.

Once you've got a handle on how long tasks take you, you're ready to start planning your days to get the most out of them. Here's my tips on writing an organized to-do list!

TOP TIPS: HOW TO WRITE A TO-DO LIST

What do your to-do lists look like? Are they a rough scribble of important tasks, or are they 20 items deep? It's taken me a while to perfect my to-do list game, but now I love them.

One tip I love from Sarah Knight's brilliant book, *How to Get Your S**t Together*, is to stop writing endlessly long to-do lists. Rather than writing a 'To-Do' list, instead write a 'Must Do' list, that's no longer than five items. On this list, you write everything that's totally urgent for the day ahead – the things you really can't put off for a minute longer – and make sure those are your priority for the day ahead.

The idea being that with longer to-do lists, we allow ourselves to slip into a habit of doing the easiest tasks first and putting off the things that are really important. This method allows you to focus and concentrate on the urgent matters at hand, cutting through the noise of what you *could* be doing, and focusing on what you *should* be doing.

Going a step further, I then like to write sub-headings for my to-do lists, so that they are grouped by projects. I find otherwise I jump from task to task during the day, and skip too much between different projects, not feeling like I'm getting further with anything at all! If you're an entrepreneur with several projects on the go, you might find it easier to group your tasks by project too.

Here's an example of what a daily to-do list looks like for me:

IMPORTANT

List five things that have to get done today.

IF TIME...

About Time Academy

(List five key tasks below.)

#SheStartedIt Podcast

(List five key tasks below.)

Freelance Writing

(List five key tasks below.)

Of course, we all wish that we had more time. Technology is a great way to automate elements of your business and work. And, of course, if there are things that are taking up lots of your time that you really don't enjoy, look to hire someone who can relieve the workload for you. Maybe you need a bookkeeper, so you can free up more time for things in your business you do enjoy?

TOP TIPS: AUTOMATING YOUR WORK

↳ First, **set up smart labels** in Gmail or rules in Outlook to automatically sort emails you receive, based on sender or keywords.

↳ Set up **suggested responses** in Gmail (such as 'sounds good!'), so you're not wasting time typing.

↳ Use **Boomerang**, a Gmail plugin, to schedule email responses, so you don't need to remember to follow up.

↳ Use browser extensions like **Grammarly** to auto-correct your spelling and grammar mistakes in real life, to save you time proof-reading.

↳ Set up **Google alerts** for any news stories you're keeping on top of, to save you time scouring the news every morning.

↪ **Auto-chase invoices** using accounting software. Subscriptions such as QuickBooks or Xero are great for automating your banking. You can set them to auto-chase invoices that are overdue, so you don't have to.

↪ Set up **standing orders**. Make sure to set up any standing orders for people you regularly pay the same amount, to save time on online banking.

↪ Create team to-do lists with **Trello**. For team projects, you might want to set up a Trello board – this is a great way to keep track of everyone's progress without having to check in.

↪ Use **Dropbox** to save all your receipts. Take a quick snap on your phone of your receipt and upload it to Dropbox – this will save you time rooting around for old receipts around the house!

Understanding your productivity blocks

Be mindful of the things that hinder your productivity. We're all guilty of spending too much time on our phones during the workday – I find it much easier to focus with my phone switched to airplane mode, especially when doing anything creative.

Technology is designed to suck us in – it's frictionless and all too consuming. We have to actively fight against a million distractions during the day. If you're interested in detoxing from your phone generally, Catherine Gray's *How to Break Up with Your Phone* is a fantastic book about our relationship with technology.

Distractions don't make us happy. We might feel a quick dopamine hit from Instagram stories, but what makes us truly, deeply content is being fulfilled by our work. Allowing interferences to crowd out our working day will lead to a cycle of frustration and disappointment in ourselves. Productivity = fulfilment. Do more of what makes *you* happy.

Need some more inspiration? I asked a clinical psychotherapist for her top tips on overcoming digital distractions at the end of this chapter.

WORKBOOK

Q1: When are you most productive? Morning and night? When is your energy highest?

_____

_____

_____

Q2: What makes you more productive? How can you fit more of this into your day?

_____

_____

_____

_____

Q3: How good are you at planning out the day ahead? How can you be more organized at work?

_____

_____

_____

_____

Q4: What tasks do you find yourself doing multiple times during the week? How can you batch these to be more productive?

_____

_____

_____

_____

Q5: What are your biggest distractions at work? What three actionable steps can you take to limit these distractions?

_____

_____

_____

_____

Q6: What's stopping you from being your most efficient self?

_____

_____

_____

_____

CASE STUDY   She Made It: Dr Kirren Schnack

Name: Dr Kirren Schnack
Job title: Clinical psychologist

How would you describe our relationship with technology?

Technology has become indispensable to us in our everyday life. We get so much, so easily, at our fingertips – a phone, a camera, a multimedia player, internet browsing, shopping, a navigation system, email service, social networking, playing games, using fitness apps, and endless other applications that appeal to our daily habits.

We have all, to varying degrees, become too dependent on our technology. Even though technology has improved the quality of life, our behaviour and relationship to our devices has become an epidemic in modern society. We start the day looking at our phone, maybe to turn off the alarm, then we're tempted to have a quick look at our notifications, while we eat breakfast, on our commute, in our breaks, on the loo, whilst waiting in the supermarket, whilst waiting for literally anything. If we lose our phone, it's as if an integral part of our being has been lost.

What effect is our relationship with technology having on our sense of self?

Despite the advantages associated with technology, research suggests that many of us overuse technology in ways that interfere with our daily lives, safety, health, mental health and behavioural choices.

It changes our attitudes towards ourselves and towards others, negatively affects our work, our social interaction, and is associated with a number of psychological disorders. Our sense of self can take a real battering from having an unhealthy relationship with our phones – studies show that low self-esteem is linked to a higher use of technology.

For women in particular, the social comparison has emerged as more prominent than for men. We ask so much of social media; we want validation, feelings of self-worth and self-integrity, and quality interactions. But in reality, we don't always get these responses – and compare ourselves with others who do. It's useful to reflect on this: who were we, and how did we view ourselves, before our technology use became unhealthy?

How do you know you're addicted to your phone?

As medical and psychological experts, we are reluctant to assign the word 'addiction' to anything other than an actual substance. The only addiction that is behavioural and has behavioural similarities with the overuse of technology is compulsive gambling. The common similarities that show we have an unhealthy dependence on technology are:

↪ **Loss of control** over our use – we try to limit it, or say we should, but don't succeed in doing so.

↪ **Persistence** – we continually engage in the behaviour – whether it be taking selfies, checking email, or compulsively scrolling through Instagram, and this persistent use is characterized by a sense of loss of time.

↪ **Tolerance** – we have a need to engage in the behaviour more frequently to get some kind of satisfaction, and might find ourselves mindlessly grabbing our technology/device even when we don't really need to.

↪ **Severe negative consequences** stemming from the behaviour – it might be that we start to compare ourselves with others, leading to self-hatred, anxiety, social-media depression. Or it keeps us awake, causing insomnia, it gets in the way of relationships, makes us late for work and so forth.

↪ **Withdrawal**, or feelings of irritability and anxiety when we can't engage in the behaviour – perhaps when we have lost, forgotten or broken a device, and the desperation we then suffer.

↪ **Relapse**, or picking up the habit again after short periods of avoidance – you might decide to limit your use for a few days, but then pick it back up after just two days.

↪ **Preoccupation** – we are occupied with the content we have seen on our device. It might be something in an email, the perfect interior, the perfect body – whatever it is, it plays on our mind, intruding on our thoughts.

Look at whether your use affects how you feel – including feeling angry, sad, anxious, tense, and irritable. Are you turning to your phone when experiencing unwanted feelings, such as anxiety or depression?

How important is it to step away from tech and social media regularly?

It is important to establish and learn to maintain boundaries around technology use. When we do this regularly we can get into a habit of positive limit-setting, which is great for our mental health. We sleep better, do more, engage in life differently, feel happier, experience less problematic emotions, feel more in control of ourselves and feel more free.

What are your top tips for detoxing from tech?

1 Turn off all instant notifications on at least some days of the week, or maybe at certain times, so they don't serve as a distraction to pull you back in.

2 Designate time in the day (every day) that is technology-free. This might be when you get home until after dinner, or between dinner and bedtime, or another time.

3 Decide when you would really like to use and not use your phone. Would you really like to look at your phone first thing bleary eyed, or

would it suit you better to look at it once you've enjoyed your morning getting ready and are now on your commute? If so, again set a time to use the technology accordingly.

4 If you're concerned that time will get away with you, set a timer as you grab your technology, with full intention of how long you actually want to spend on your phone – 15 minutes? 30 minutes?

5 Designate whole weekends, or a whole week, where you don't use any unnecessary technology, and on those days plan alternative activities for yourself.

What are some of the best ways that we reconnect with the real world?

To start with, stop using your technology for the last hour or two before bed; instead choose another activity that feeds you – maybe that's reading, yoga, drawing, or writing a gratitude journal. Spend some time thinking about things you really love to do, but haven't been able to – maybe it's as simple as taking a walk to watch the sunset, or planning to reconnect with an old friend. Once you have identified at least five of these, get scheduling – when can you do them? How can you make these a regular part of your routine so they bring you balance? Use this method to keep engaged with real life, and live a real life alongside your life with technology.

How important is digital detoxing for entrepreneurs?

A digital detox is not easy for the online entrepreneur. While running a business it can feel like there is a constant need to be connected: you want to succeed, you want to respond to emails instantly, deal with messages and comments, keep your social media updated – after all, it's all part of the job. It's important to get the balance right between stepping away from technology and feeling cut off from your work. Entrepreneurs need to achieve this balance much more, given that they usually spend a lot more time using technology. It can become all-consuming.

Any tips for digital hygiene for entrepreneurs?

It can help to try and allot a specific number of hours in the day for emails or social media, taking half an hour off to read a book or go for a walk. If your email has a pause function, use it so that you don't get distracted away from your goals. You can also use the flight mode for a couple of hours. Consider taking small but regular chunks of time off, where you are 'out of office' with all cellular data switched off whilst you dive/swim/hike…

Tips for boosting productivity and removing distractions during the working day?

Turning off all notifications on technology devices during set periods of the day will enhance productivity, as will putting devices in another room, or placing them into flight mode. We are also less likely to be affected by distractions if we have a clear plan for the day. Planning your day and prioritizing your tasks is the difference between having a reactive day and a proactive day. Begin your day with your most critical tasks first. By planning your day the night before (or early in the morning), you can prioritize your workflow. Being intentional with your time and where you spend it can enhance productivity, as well as allow you to build in breaks and quality recharges.

Here are three simple questions to ask yourself each day/evening to help productivity:

1 Which task will make me feel the most accomplished today?

2 Which actions/tasks will I take today that move me in the direction of my longer-term goals?

3 What's the value/emotion in getting this done, and what's the risk if I don't?

Dr Kirren Schnack is a Clinical Psychologist based in Oxford; find her on Instagram or visit her website: https://drschnack.com

CHAPTER SEVEN

How to find your inner boss

Here's a question: are you ready to lead? One of the hardest aspects of running your own business is leading people. Whilst the challenges you face running a small business are different from those in a big corporate, understanding what leadership means to you will benefit you, no matter what age or stage of your career.

We need to be doing more to encourage female leadership at every level. According to Women Count 2020, FTSE 350 companies which have executive committees with female membership of more than 33 per cent have a net profit margin over 10 times greater than those companies with no women at this level. And yet, in 2020, there are just 13 women CEOs of FTSE 350 companies.[1]

For some, leadership comes naturally. They step into their role as a leader and feel confident steering the ship, managing others and creating an inspiring place to work. For others, leadership is a skill that needs to be learned.

Don't worry if it takes you time to find your own leadership style – leading others is an ever-evolving process. Nobody is born the perfect leader; for me, discovering my own personal style came out of trial and error. It starts with making a commitment to yourself and others that you're always willing to improve.

I've learned that good leadership = *compassionate* leadership – creating a space where people feel valued, seen and heard. The most enjoyable work environments, ones where people show up as their best selves, ready to seize the day and excel professionally, are ones where everyone feels respected and appreciated.

Being a leader doesn't mean being the loudest person in the room: leadership is about listening. It means being someone that your team always feel they can approach, talk openly and honestly with, and come away feeling heard.

Leadership is also about action – knowing when change needs to take place in the workplace and not being afraid of having difficult conversations. To that end, leadership is the confidence to make decisions, take action and show an unwavering commitment to lead a team even through the most challenging times.

CASE STUDY   She Made It: Women in leadership roles

Leadership is particularly interesting in the context of female-owned businesses. From my experience, female founders are often more concerned about *how* they appear as a leader than men. Being nice and wanting to be 'liked' is often in conflict with being respected.

I know that you can be both liked AND respected, but it can sometimes feel like the two are at odds with each other. I fear women care about being liked more than their male counterparts, and that in itself holds women back from reaching their higher potential.

Many women are frustrated that leadership often feels like it's competing with being popular. I know from experience that allowing the distinction between work and personal relationship slide too much is a difficult position to come back from. It's hard to lead people you've become very good friends with. Part of the role of a leader is to create boundaries – ones that allow you to lead with authority and respect, and give you space to properly manage people.

We know there are still so many barriers to women reaching senior leadership positions. According to Women Count 2020, it's largely women who are helping women – companies in the FTSE 350 led by women have an average of one in three female executive committee members, which falls to an average of one in five for companies led by men.[2] I believe the boom in female entrepreneurship is partly due to this frustration in not being able to climb to the senior position in big corporates. More women are choosing to go it alone, start their own companies and give themselves a leadership role from the start.

What's brilliant about the rise in female entrepreneurship is that we ourselves have the power to create the future of work for women. Entrepreneurship gives an amazing space and ability to create the company you truly want to work in. It's a blank slate – where *you* create the company culture, ethos and vision – and that's an exciting challenge!

Want to create good vibes from the top down? Here are some top tips on effective leadership from Maggie O'Carroll, CEO of The Women's Organisation:

Diversity first

Whilst it goes without saying that we need more women in leadership roles, valuing diversity does not end with gender. Cultivate a diverse workforce that includes people of varying age, religion, race, ethnicity, cultural background, sexual orientation, socioeconomic status and language. Ensure that there's a seat at the table for them. As a leader, you should value the opinions and contributions of those who are different from you and understand that their lived experience is vital to your decision-making. Diversity should be engrained into the fabric of your business – live and breathe it.

Establish your expertise

Whatever industry you work in, establish yourself as an expert in that field. Be the go-to person that others associate with a service, product or subject. Say yes to profiling opportunities, whether it's press or events, and speak with clarity, conviction and confidence on the matters that are important to you and your business. Have the patience and dedication to build a network of advocates who trust and respect your expertise – opportunities will follow. Increasing your profile also helps the people you lead – it creates more trust and authority with your audience.

Create change

Getting political is about leading the way for change. If you feel frustrated at decisions being made locally and nationally that affect your business and community, get involved and be a part of the solution. A leader will listen to the concerns of their network and be proactive in vocalizing those concerns to ensure their community is recognized at the highest levels. Understand who the key decision-makers are in relation to your agenda and work with them to drive mutually beneficial impact.

Pioneer and pave

It is well documented that women are massively under-represented in senior positions. If you're a woman in a leadership role, recognize that you're a pioneer and begin to pave the way for others. To achieve a more balanced and equal economy, we need to ensure the door remains open for more women to succeed. Look within your own network and nurture those who will be the leaders of tomorrow – recognize your power and use your sphere of influence to change the status quo.

Celebrate your success

Since 1996, The Women's Organisation has worked with women to develop their roles in all aspects of society. Whatever their background, a consistent commonality for women is dealing with a lack of confidence. Women do vital work in all areas of business, politics and in the wider community – let's start talking about it. One of the biggest sources of inspiration to anyone wanting to achieve something is seeing someone like them who has been there and done it too. Believe in the power of role models and recognize that you are one. Be bold, step into the spotlight and tell your story.

Wondering where to start on your leadership journey? It can be overwhelming for first-time leaders, so here are my thoughts on the key fundamentals:

Leadership: it all starts with you

So much of leadership is bound up in self-confidence. To be a good leader, you need to start with the individual. Business is all about belief – believing in your product, service and yourself – and radiating that energy of self-confidence to inspire others.

If you're doubting yourself, you're not in the strongest position to lead. As Michelle Obama said to a group of young girls in London in 2009, 'Whether you come from a council estate or a country estate, your success will be determined by your own confidence and fortitude.'[3] Positive role models set the tone for your whole company – and compassionate leadership should be at the core of any successful business.

Understanding what makes you feel strong, empowered and confident is the beginning of your journey towards being a leader. Invest in things that boost your self-confidence – whether that's gym classes, work clothes or a professional coach.

Leadership: invest in yourself

If you're lacking confidence in leadership, maybe it's about time to invest in yourself. Learning and development is a great way to continually challenge and push yourself as a leader – I've found having coaches and mentors along the way have really accelerated my entrepreneurial journey.

Try not to see it as an outgoing – investing in your personal development and growth is one of the best things you can do for the long-term health of your company. Financial investment in yourself now is also investment in your future; don't be afraid to spend money on yourself and give yourself new tools to develop as a leader.

Personally, I've found coaching that involves a lot of visualization techniques to be really impactful for my leadership skills. Neuro-linguistic programming (NLP), in particular, is an effective way to work through mental blocks around leadership and build self-confidence. NLP is a psychological approach that involves analysing strategies used by successful individuals and applying them to reach a personal goal.

Professional leadership courses are a great way to invest in yourself. Look for local courses in your area or check out some of the amazing online ones on offer. The most important thing with coaching is to dedicate ample time to do the 'homework'. Coaching can be an amazing tool, but the real impact of it will only be felt if you put in as much time as possible.

CASE STUDY   She Made It: Sophie Edmond

Name: Sophie Edmond
Job title: Women's leadership strategist and founder of The Art of Women's Leadership

What are the most common blocks that hold women back in leadership?

In my experience, the most common thing that holds women back is themselves!

When it comes to their careers, women tend to be less deliberate. They are four times less likely to leave their current employer for an opportunity than men, who tend to have a planned career path and take action to move along it.

Women tend to put less emphasis on networking and spend much less time doing it. This is partly because of caring responsibility – many networking events take place after work hours. Women are more comfortable in formal professional relationships, such as mentoring and having sponsors. When it comes to less formal interactions, women have a significant disadvantage, as this informal style often lays the seeds for future opportunities.

What effect do care roles have on leadership?

Women have to contend with juggling work and home life. Historically, women have owned more of the caring responsibilities and this can lead to them curbing their ambitions and turning down opportunities because of the impact on their families.

Generally speaking, women believe their work and CV should speak *for* them. As a result, they dedicate less time to identifying and creating their unique value proposition.

They need to develop their skills in crafting their success stories that speak to their capabilities and the value they bring. It's about telling their story to the right people.

How do you discover your own personal style of leadership?

Self-awareness is a key component of discovering your personal style of leadership. To raise your levels of self-awareness:

↪ Identify and know your strengths.

↪ Reflect on your mistakes and learn from them.

↪ Seek feedback from people you trust.

↪ Decide how to mitigate your weaknesses and build a workaround.

↪ Make a decision and commitment to change.

Can you learn to be a leader?

Yes! You can certainly learn to lead through a number of different ways – the first one is making a decision to lead, as it's not for everyone.

As a leader, you have to show your humanity, which means communication, listening and demonstrating compassion. You also have to create a culture where people *want* to follow you – to be followers. Research from the Gallup Organization found that followers need trust, stability, hope and compassion from great leaders.

These values are crucial for leading teams; people need to be able to trust you and each other and, above all, you need to be able to trust them.

It's about creating a space where people feel they can speak up and challenge other team members without criticism.

How do you overcome your inner critic to lead with confidence?

Imposter syndrome, which is described as 'the persistent inability to believe that one's success is deserved or has been legitimately achieved as a result of one's own efforts or skills', is much more prevalent for women than for men. Symptoms include low self-confidence, fear of failure and being found out as a fraud.

The inner critic is a phenomenon created in our minds – it's not based on facts. Here are five ways to overcome it:

TOP TIPS: HOW TO OVERCOME IMPOSTER SYNDROME

1 Recognize and acknowledge it. Try to talk about it with others, and remember, you're not alone.
2 Separate feelings from facts. Sometimes we make mistakes and feel stupid – it's human nature.
3 Think about your strengths and achievements and write them out. We all forget about some of the amazing things we as individuals have created or been recognized for. Go right back to your childhood, think about your personal and professional lives and look at the list regularly. Think about what you've overcome in your life to get to where you are.
4 Develop a new script. If we tell ourselves that we're no good at something, we will believe that and act accordingly.

---

5 Visualize and reward success – imagine what it feels like to be successful at something. It creates warm and fuzzy feelings, which are certainly more pleasant than stomach-turning fear and anxiety. Reward yourself regularly for recognizing imposter syndrome and for overcoming it. Treat yourself.

What are your top tips for boosting self-confidence?

Taking yourself out of your comfort zone is a great way to boost confidence. Once we step out of the comfort zone, we enter the fear zone (where we'll make excuses for not doing something!). Having pushed through this, we enter the learning zone, where we deal with challenges presented to us, and ultimately, we will land at the growth zone, where we find purpose and conquer our objectives.

In the next chapter, we're going to be looking at potential pitfalls with being self-employed and discover how to set yourself up for success mentally.

Leadership: make it your own

One of the challenges about being a leader is removing some of the limiting beliefs in your own head about what leadership 'should' look like. Leadership is no longer a traditional top–down approach, where companies are run by CEOs in glass offices, that feel far removed from their employees. A more democratic, open style of leadership is evolving where – like the open-plan office space itself – leadership looks and feels more informal than ever before.

Millennials, in particular, are put off by companies where leadership seems to be too formal or rigid, and start-up culture, where everyone has their say and companies are led with a less hierarchical approach, is infiltrating even the most traditional corporate companies.

The new era of business is about leaders who are relaxed, approachable, open and honest – these are the leaders of today, who convey confidence, passion and enthusiasm to their workforce.

EXERCISE: DISCOVERING YOUR INNER LEADER

Here's a short exercise to get you familiar with your natural leadership qualities:

Write a list of all the qualities you think a leader should have.

Write a list of the qualities you see in yourself.

Now remember a time when you displayed the leadership qualities above. When was the last time you felt yourself embody those skills?

Internalize that feeling – write down the memory – and remind yourself of it whenever you're feeling doubtful or uncertain.

Hopefully in this chapter you've learned new things about your own leadership style and feel more confident and ready to lead! Next up, we'll be looking at managing stress when self-employed.

WORKBOOK

Q1: Who are the leaders who inspire you most and why? List three things you admire in them.

_____

_____

_____

_____

Q2: What kind of managerial style do you wish to adopt? How would you like others to feel when they are managed by you?

_____

_____

_____

_____

Q3: What are you most afraid of when leading? How can you build confidence in those areas? List three actionable steps.

_____

_____

_____

_____

Q4: What qualities do you think you possess that will make you a great authority in your field? How can you remind yourself regularly of your own abilities?

_____

_____

_____

_____

CASE STUDY   She Made It: Becci Martin

Name: Becci Martin
Job title: Director at Boo Coaching and Consulting Limited

How did you get into the work you're doing now?

I'm a mental health nurse by background and I have always been passionate about supporting people to learn and grow – I wanted to be a teacher when I was at school! I launched Boo Coaching and Consulting in August 2012 and it has grown over the years to deliver leadership, coaching and workplace wellbeing programmes across the UK. We help to create healthy and happy workplaces through helping bosses to be better bosses (we have all had or known a bad boss) and we do this with a consistent focus on creating social value in all we do.

I took redundancy from my role in the NHS soon after having my daughter and stepped into a new sector to take a peek over the fence! That step gave me the courage I needed to head into self-employment and later launching the company. If I am honest, I really wanted to create a workplace where I felt at home, where I had an opportunity to create bigger ripples within society. The traditional office culture was stressful and at the time I didn't feel supported as a new mother, working full-time and experiencing all the mental health issues that went along with a complicated mix of stress and lack of self-care.

What was the inspiration behind the company?

I really wanted to create an organization that proves that we can do business differently! My vision is to be a globally recognized company, helping leaders to be amazing, and we do that through delivering in line with our values. We can all tell a story about a bad boss or a tricky workplace scenario where we didn't feel supported, but I wanted to shift the narrative so more people could start to talk about great bosses and the positive impact they had on their lives and careers – work can be wonderful and life-enhancing.

When it comes to company culture, where do you begin? How do you create an inclusive, happy place to work?

One of the biggest impacts on our wellbeing at work is how we are led and how this makes us feel. At Boo we spend most of our time helping bosses to be better bosses, so it is important that I get this right. We recruit on values and develop skills needed. It all comes down to bringing kind and compassionate folk together to do great work that has an impact on society. We are a mentally healthy workplace and members of the Good Business Charter – this stuff really matters to us.

I trust my team to do their jobs. I haven't suddenly just decided to trust them; we have worked on this from the moment each member of my team joined Boo. Creating trust and psychological safety are at the heart of excellent leadership, and I know that I work more effectively and am far more creative when I am trusted to deliver and not micro-managed within an inch of my life.

We have taken the time to create the best conditions for our team to thrive over the last few years. Understanding each other's values and strengths is a brilliant starting point. However, technology has really helped us to build connection in recent years. Communicating with each member of my team has varied and is driven by what they need, their working hours and what work they are focused on.

Have you found anything that really works for your company culture?

It's all about kindness! Recruit kind people who demonstrate similar values to those of your company, create the conditions for all to thrive and build trust from day one. Help everyone to focus on their strengths and give everyone a chance to shine … if there's an idea – try it out!

What does a diverse workforce actually mean to you?

A diverse workforce is one which represents the communities and customers we serve. Recruiting kind people who care about our customers and understand the complexities within society really does make a difference – build a workforce that is able to challenge inequality and injustice and reflects society. For me this means offering properly flexible working conditions, an unlimited paid time off policy and full support when life is tough.

Any dos and don'ts for leadership?

A tip that I share with leaders on our coaching skills development programme is to simply ask your team what style helps bring out the best in them. Don't try and figure it out on your own – ask people what they need, but don't be afraid to be directive if the situation requires it. The trick here is to flex your approach depending on the situation, the needs of your colleagues and the knowledge and skills they have. I sometimes share the coaching continuum and ask what style suits them best.

I don't always get this right! I need my team to tell me honestly if I have missed an opportunity to properly support them – I know I can revert to my happy coaching place when I really should be more *tell*.

Again, spend time creating the right conditions for your team to thrive, but if you are in a hurry and are managing newly formed teams in this current situation, simply ask them what style of leadership gets the best out of them and do that.

Any advice for aspiring entrepreneurs who want to be better leaders?

Get yourself a mentor, ask lots of questions and work on your inner critic! Dial that mean voice back and be your true self – please don't force yourself to fit some old-fashioned leadership trope. Work on your emotional intelligence and make career choices based on your values.

What does modern-day leadership for women look like?

Modern-day leadership looks messy and exciting and challenging and complicated, but rewarding as hell when you get it right. There is no one-size-fits-all and so there is no textbook answer I can give here – all I can say is that it is based around creating the best conditions for everyone else to thrive and looking after yourself as best you can throughout.

CHAPTER EIGHT

How to manage stress, burnout and founder fatigue

L et's talk about stress. What is stress? Does running a business *need* to be stressful?

We all have our personal experience of stress; it might manifest physically, such as anxiety, hyper-activity or difficulty sleeping, or it might be felt mentally, such as racing thoughts, inability to concentrate or even depression. The worrying thing about stress is how prevalent low-level, constant pressure is in the digital age – whether it's another email that needs answering, something else you *should* be doing or feeling the need to constantly check social media. It can be incredibly hard to get off the hamster wheel of constantly being 'on'.

So far, we've looked at organization, mindset and understanding your skill set, which all contribute to your general grip on your business and your resilience in tackling difficulties, so in this chapter we're going to focus on some practical things you can do to reduce your feelings of stress.

Founder fatigue: why does it happen?

Running a business comes with many more challenges than a conventional 9–5 office job might. If you're a 'solopreneur', you might be single-handedly in charge of finances, making sure cash is always coming in and invoices are paid on time. Whilst you may be able to alleviate some of the pressure by hiring an accountant in time, the founder always feels financial stress more keenly. After all, your business is your baby, and whatever happens to it affects you personally too.

Beyond the weight of the admin involved in running a business, there's also a pressure on people management. As discussed in the previous chapter, company culture and leadership are some of the most important things about growing and sustaining your business. Founder fatigue can be felt from the sheer pressure of dealing with people – looking after their wellbeing, career progression and job satisfaction – on top of everything.

I'm saying these things not to put you off running your own business, but just to make you aware that it's totally *normal* to feel pressure as a founder. In fact, it's a sign that you're passionate and you care about the project.

There are practical things you can do to alleviate founder pressure, but many of these involve delegation and hiring, which I know isn't always possible at the start when budgets are tight. If you're doing mostly everything yourself right now, know that as your business and income grow, you'll be able to lift some of that pressure by having others to take over responsibility.

As we'll see a lot in this book, imposter syndrome seems to be rife with female founders. If it's your first company or you're launching something brand new, you might be experiencing a lot of self-doubt, which contributes to a feeling of stress. Stepping away from self-doubt and silencing your inner critic will benefit you in the long run: the real, tangible stresses of a business are enough; you don't need to pile additional stress on yourself with negative self-talk.

Managing stress as a first-time founder

There's so much I've learned about how to reduce your stress levels in the early stages of running your own business! Here are a few practical steps you can take to feel more control:

Don't just learn on the job

Stress for first-time founders is often rooted in feeling unprepared. So, put yourself in the driving seat and take control of your work by committing to further education.

Courses, training and seminars are a great way to support your entrepreneurial journey. In my first year of business, I took short courses at City Lit in London – they are inexpensive and accessible after work, offering everything from bookkeeping to business plans. Find local or online courses on the topics that you feel most overwhelmed by and make learning a lifelong process.

Create a proper structure

Structure is incredibly important; it gives you a sense of stability, ownership and control. It sets the tone for your day and sets you up for productivity and success.

It's very easy when you're newly self-employed to go into free-fall with your structure – working all hours, without a dedicated workspace and burning out.

When I first launched my business, I would work until 2am and wake up feeling incredibly groggy, and then guilt myself for having a slow morning and find myself working late into the evening to make up time – and the cycle would continue.

Be strict with yourself on your structure – treat working for yourself as you would in any other company. Start early morning, give yourself an hour for lunch, an afternoon break, and shut your laptop as early as possible and allow yourself the whole night off.

Learn to disconnect

Burnout, a state of emotional, physical, and mental exhaustion caused by excessive and prolonged stress, is often caused by feeling like you never have any time off. And I don't just mean *taking* time off, but actually fully switching off your mind.

This is easier said than done. Especially in startup culture, I feel like we're always on. You have to be strict with yourself if you're going to truly disconnect. If you allow work to fill your every moment, you'll never feel fully off.

I think it's because, in many ways, with startups we've come to glamourize being busy – more and more founders are burning out because they place work above everything else in their lives. This top-heavy culture means that there's little space for down time, and even when you are truly relaxed, work consumes your thoughts. It's actually not healthy and learning to mentally switch off will help you – we need to break the long-hours culture as a badge of honour!

Take up hobbies!

Hobbies are a great way to de-stress – especially anything that takes you away from your screen for long periods. Getting out into nature as much as possible, connecting with your creative side and generally creating space in your life for things that make you feel calm and connected are super important. Don't let the business be the only thing in your life; it's a sure-fire way to head towards burnout.

Support yourself

I don't think I would have survived the first year of business without amazing people around me. Every entrepreneur needs to find their 'tribe' – people that can support, encourage and inspire you. There's going to be a lot of storms to weather and that is *a lot* easier to do with a tribe around you.

Being a founder can be a lonely journey. Here are some ways you can alleviate loneliness and create a support system around you and your business:

↪ **Hire people,** as soon as you can afford to. Work out what the most crucial hire would be for your business and bring on someone that can support your vision.
↪ **Get a co-founder** if it suits your business plan. The co-founder relationship is not for everyone, but a business partner may be a great way to join forces and support each other.
↪ **Create a network** that supports you – whether that's friends, family or colleagues. Hold space in your life for people that believe in and encourage you, don't let negativity infiltrate your work too much.
↪ **Take on a business mentor.** Paying a professional mentor or coach can be a great way to talk through your journey and feel held throughout.
↪ **Join an online community** to find like-minded individuals. Beyond social media networks, there are plenty of great platforms designed specifically for female entrepreneurs.

What to look for in a co-founder

The co-founder relationship is a special one – and it's very important you get it right. The decision to take on a co-founder is a huge one – and can be a determining factor in the success of your business. Finding someone who can complement your skill set is a real plus. Alexandra Depledge and Jules Coleman were best friends who co-founded Resi, having sold their previous business Hassle for £27.5 million. On the co-founder relationship, they were quoted in an interview with Business Cloud saying:

> You can pretty much split the company in half: Jules takes anything that's quite detailed and logical – such as tech, products and finance – and I tend to take the people side of stuff such as marketing and sales, operations and financing.

Here are some more things to look for in a co-founder:

↳ **Complementary skill set** – you want someone whose skills complement, not conflict with, yours. Be wary that you're not competing over the same roles. For example, if you have a more creative flair, you may look for a co-founder who has a keen eye for numbers or logistics.

↳ **Alignment of vision and values** – this is a very important process for co-founders to work through. Do you share a common vision for the business? Do you hold the same values? Jotting down your vision and values and comparing notes may save you a lot of stress down the line.

↳ **Flexibility** – are you flexible and fluid in your approach, and would you like a co-founder who is similar? If one of you has a more set approach, it may cause conflict.

↳ **Openness and communication skills** – any ability to communicate effectively is crucial with co-founders. This may be the most important relationship you have, so it needs to function as effectively as a romantic relationship would. Make sure you're both people who will express concerns, talk calmly and be solution-focused in thinking.

↳ **Similar attitudes to money and work ethic** – two big problems I've seen in co-founder relationships is differing attitudes to spending and work ethic. These are two very important attitudes in a business – and it can create a lot of tensions – so have these discussions before entering into an agreement.

WORKBOOK

Q1: How much do you know about the business you're about to run? How much do you have left to learn? How can you learn more?

_____

_____

_____

_____

Q2: How can you create a sense of structure to your working day?

_____

_____

_____

_____

Q3: How can you bring more people in to share your vision? Who will be your first hire?

_____

_____

_____

_____

Q4: Who are the people who bring a sense of companionship to your work? Who supports you?

_____

_____

_____

_____

Q5: What areas do you need the most support in? How can you get supported more?

_____

_____

_____

_____

Q6: What are the things that you love, which calm and relax you? List three activities that you love and try to do them once a week.

_____

_____

_____

_____

Q7: How can you disconnect more? List three habits that can help you take a break from technology and work.

_____

_____

_____

_____

CASE STUDY   She Made It: Chloe Brotheridge

Name: Chloe Brotheridge
Job title: Hypnotherapist, coach and author

How did you get into the work you're doing now?

I started my career as a nutritionist in the NHS, then retrained as a hypnotherapist in 2011. I've since studied coaching and NLP and combine all three in my sessions. Since having anxiety myself, I specialize in helping others with anxiety and wrote my book _The Anxiety Solution_ in 2017.

What are your biggest learnings about stress and anxiety through your work?

I think stress and anxiety are normal responses to the world we live in and the sort of lives we lead. There's so much pressure and everything is happening so fast. We need to counteract this by having tools in place to help us to stay calm. If you don't have time to meditate, you must have a lot of time to feel like sh*t.

When it comes to stress, what are some of the most common stressors for entrepreneurs?

Things I see the most are: never feeling like you're 'doing' enough, having no work–life balance and self-doubt.

What are your top three practical tips for entrepreneurs to overcome stress?

↳ Remember that resting and taking breaks will improve your productivity and motivation.

↳ Most people experience self-doubt and imposter syndrome – it's a normal side effect of going outside of your comfort zone, doing something new and growing as a person.

↳ There are no prizes for being the busiest, most burned-out person. Focus on the 20 per cent of business activities that give you 80 per cent of the results.

How do you set up your work and life in a balanced way when you're self-employed?

For me personally, this is what helps:

↳ I meditate twice a day, morning and evening, to start the day well and then to switch off.

↳ I delete Instagram from my phone when I want to spend less time on it.

↳ I book in two days a week for admin and creative work and have no calls or clients on those days. It's much more chill.

Is anxiety something we 'overcome' or something we learn to live with?

Anxiety isn't something you have; it's something you experience and our experiences always change. We can reduce our anxiety and learn to handle situations better so it's no longer so bad that it holds us back.

What does a healthy daily routine look like?

I get up early and go to bed at 9:30pm ideally! I love to practise qi gong – I'm convinced it's helped my immune system. I'm trying to get into green tea but I'm really sensitive to caffeine. I have a much happier relationship with my partner when we go for a walk together every day so I'm doing that too.

How can you train yourself to be more positive and productive for the workday ahead?

I ask myself, 'What would make today great?' That might mean calling a friend, doing some exercise, taking time away from my desk to stretch. I look at cute dog videos on Instagram. I burn some incense and say some prayers.

What are five things anyone can do to create a calmer you?

↪ When you've experienced something stressful, get up and shake your body for 30 seconds or more. It discharges tension and adrenaline.

↪ Remember that you can't be everyone's cup of tea. You can't please everyone and that is okay.

↪ Learn to be kind to yourself. It's one of the most important things you can do for yourself. It comes with practice. Keep reminding yourself to speak to yourself as you would a friend.

↪ 'If you win the rat race, you'll still be a rat.' What makes you happy and brings you joy? Don't wait until you've achieved a milestone to feel joyful; go and do what makes you feel good now. We never know how much time we have left.

↪ Seek therapy or coaching if you're struggling. You're worthy of getting help and support, and feeling anxious is not inevitable for you. Anxiety can get worse unless we get help. It's better to nip it in the bud than let it spiral.

PART TWO

All about your business

The first part of *She Made It* addressed your personal mindset, vision and leadership style, which all play a crucial part in growing a successful business. I hope you've now put yourself in the driving seat of your business and discovered the attitude to give yourself the best chance of success.

In this second part, we're going to be looking at the finer details of the business you're going to run, including business models, investment and finance, and strategic hiring. For me, business is about the alchemy between emotional resilience, entrepreneurial mindset and important practical considerations, such as money, problem-solving and growth strategy.

In Part Three of the book I'm going to be giving you a 'toolkit' that you can use to amplify and rapidly grow your business, including strategies for boosting your social media, personal brand, PR and community.

First, the most important thing is starting the *right* business. You may have a calling or an idea in mind, but even so, let's go back to basics to understand what the best business is for you personally.

CHAPTER NINE

How to start the right business

How can you make sure you're starting a business that's right for you?

What are the different kinds of business models available to you and what would work best around your lifestyle?

The brilliant thing about being a founder is it gives you the freedom to create a business that suits you perfectly. You're in charge of creating something that reflects your personal interests, skill set and leadership style.

In this chapter, we're going to be running through all your options, looking at the different business models, options for raising investment and financing your business and the challenges of different kinds of businesses. We'll also be getting into the nitty-gritty of cash flow in these various business types and how to write a business plan that will put you on the long-term path for success. Making sure you start the right business is so important; you want to throw yourself into something that you really feel can work in the future and pour your energy into a business that has a sustainable financial model at its core.

Starting the right business: an overview

I want to simplify the language around business in this chapter, because I know it can be intimidating when business books are heavy with jargon and terminology. In this chapter, we're going to be focusing on two different business types: service-based and product-based. Of course, your business can be a blend of the two – a service-based agency, for example, that also creates physical products. Having a basic understanding of the offerings available to you will help structure your business plan. Let's begin by looking at what you might expect with these businesses.

Service-based business

A service-based business is a commercial enterprise which provides work by an individual or team for the benefit of its customers and consumers. Typically, a service-based business provides intangible products, such as accounting, copywriting or web design, but holds no physical products or stock.

There are several benefits to service-based business, which I outline below, including low startup costs, minimal overheads and an easy route into launching. The main downside to a service-based business is manpower; growth is reliant on extra hires and staff, as these kinds of businesses require *more* people to service *more* clients.

Running a service-based business can be a balancing act with supply and demand – making sure there are enough team members to service a client, but also enough clients to justify hiring an additional financial output. You'll need to be mindful of managing income, generating new clients and using money wisely to grow.

Service-based businesses are not ones you can shortcut; they rely on a near-constant feed of new clients and maintaining existing ones to keep things flowing financially. You'll need to make sure your clients are happy with your service – and providing testimonials – and ensure your marketing strategy is strong to draw in new clients.

Examples of service-based businesses include:

↳ PR agency;
↳ business, life or career coaching;
↳ law firm;
↳ marketing or video company;
↳ make-up artist;
↳ photographer;
↳ accounting;
↳ web design, SEO or graphic design company;
↳ talent management;
↳ copywriting;
↳ personal trainer;
↳ freelance writer;
↳ influencer;
↳ chef or catering;
↳ tutoring;
↳ travel agency;
↳ cleaning company.

I think it's important to be aware of the advantages and disadvantages of the two different business styles. There might be certain things that appeal to your personal skill set and lifestyle choices more. Here are the pros and cons of service-based businesses as I see it.

Pros of service-based businesses

These are the best things about a service-based business as I see it:

↳ **Minimal capital** needed to start. You just need to be able to cover the cost of your workforce and overheads – and these costs can be even lower if you choose remote working (as so many companies are now!). You can become cash-flow positive as soon as you sign your first customer, if you're starting out as a sole owner who works from home.

↪ **Easy route** to launch – you can literally start today! You may want to put a bit of cash aside for a website, digital marketing and adverts, but the startup costs are minimal.

↪ Reduced ongoing **overheads** – you're in charge of the company's expenditure, as it's based largely on hiring. You get to decide how much cash is needed and there are fewer 'hidden' costs than in a product-based business.

↪ You may not need **financial investment** and can retain more equity in the company, as you're not buying physical stock or putting money behind research and development.

↪ More **flexibility** in setting up your work around your lifestyle – you could choose to work evenings, weekends, a few days a week or around another job.

↪ Every day is a **new day**. Service-based businesses always throw in new challenges, as you're working with different companies on rotation. Each client's needs will be different and that will keep things exciting and varied. Great for people who tire easily of doing the same tasks!

↪ This type of business is great for people who don't like **surprises!** Service-based businesses are more conventional in their working. You identify your target market, really focus in on speaking to the right audience and discover how you can promote your service best. You'll be able to earn a living by simply being good at what you do.

Cons of service-based businesses

On the flipside, there are some challenging aspects to running a service-based business. It's important that you look at both sides and think carefully about what appeals to you more:

↪ Harder to **scale**. Agencies are tricky to scale as you're charging on an hourly basis for your work, so your revenue is directly related to billable hours. This process means you have to hire more staff to deliver more services to help your business grow.

↳ Less clear-cut **pricing**. Pricing is dependent on the service you offer, but many businesses of this kind don't really know their worth and end up under-charging. There are many factors that make up your hourly fee, including all the extra admin that may go un-billed, such as emails, phone calls and additional correspondence. Try not to under-sell yourself by overlooking the actual number of hours that goes into a project – ask around your industry to get a chance of industry standard!

↳ **Lower revenue**. Although this isn't always the case with service-based businesses, payment is tied to deliverables and held within a contract. Your revenue is a reflection of the quality of your own work; thus, producing consistently good work, as the business scales, is going to be a challenge.

↳ Being **answerable**. In many ways, your creativity is capped by being client-facing. The customer is always right, and the client's vision may go against yours. You'll have to learn to deal with the opinions of others sensitively and build healthy communication into the heart of the business.

↳ **Difficult valuation**. As a service-based business doesn't hold stock or create their own products, it's harder to place a valuation on it. The worth of a service-based business is very much tied up in the team members it employs and the clients it has, which are very much personal relationships. This may prove challenging if you're ever looking to sell the business, as it could look less appealing to a potential buyer.

Who does a service-based business appeal to?

↳ People who are more risk-averse – it's easier to plan and strategize with a service-based business.

↳ People who are good at client-facing roles. You need to be a people person who's great at managing clients and juggling multiple projects.

↳ People who want to lead and manage a team. Growth in a service-based business comes from hiring – perfect for people who see themselves as a leader and want to grow a team.

↳ People who enjoy having varied working style, with lots of different clients, projects and objectives.

TOP TIPS: SEVEN WAYS TO SUPERCHARGE YOUR SERVICE-BASED BUSINESS

To supercharge your success, here are some top tips from Gemma Gilbert, a business coach for female entrepreneurs who created a six-figure business in under a year:

1 **Niche** – get clear on who you serve, the problem you solve and the result you deliver. The clearer you are on this, the easier it is for you to attract your ideal client and for your audience to easily recommend you.

2 Own your **opinions** – be a thought leader, dare to speak out and create content which actually stands out from everyone else who offers the exact same thing as you. Use content as a way of differentiating your service.

3 Invest in your **business growth** – investing money to *make* money is the best investment you can make. You'll reach your goals more quickly, and getting skin in the game will make you show up differently.

4 Lean into **fear** – fear isn't a sign to turn back and play it small. Often, it's a sign you're exactly where you should be. Use fear as your guiding compass. If it scares you, you should probably do it.

5 Work on your **mindset** daily – so many business owners think they need business strategy. In fact, they need to get out of their own way. Whether it's journaling, personal development books or meditating, make sure you work on your mindset every day.

6 Be **accountable** – whether you buddy up with a peer as an accountable partner or invest in a coach, ensure you're accountable to someone else other than yourself to reach your goals.

---

7 **Show up** consistently – motivation will come and go. Discipline needs to be a non-negotiable. Whatever channels you're using to market your business, be consistent. Don't expect your audience to show up for you if you're not showing up for them.

EXPERT GUIDE: PRICING AS A SERVICE-BASED BUSINESS

Hayley Smith is the founder of Boxed Out PR and below shares five proven methods that will help you get your pricing right and start getting paid what you're worth.

Every service business owner will go through the pain point of knowing what to charge, and what to charge for. Unlike products, which offer a tangible solution, there are a lot of factors to consider, from time, experience and skill set required:

1 **Set your price points.** Whether you offer an overall service, or various different packages, setting strong price points will help you define your offerings, create consistency and build better services. And having a good starting point and understanding the worth of the services will help you to negotiate better, and come across more confidently when selling.

2 **Be confident.** The biggest downfall when selling is a lack of confidence, especially for women. A lack of confidence will cause you to undervalue and undersell, and even if you win the business, you will walk away feeling deflated. Confidently knowing the worth of you and your services will increase your chances of success, and if they walk away, you have the satisfaction of knowing they aren't right for your business.

3 **Research your market.** But don't compare yourself with competitors. Understanding your audience will help you understand what they are looking for, and what they need, and will help you position yourself accordingly. However, even though it's useful to know what your competitors are doing, your USP is you, and that's what people are buying into, so don't feel guilty if your prices are more expensive, or your

services are more refined. You may offer a more dedicated service, or more years of experience, or even a bigger team, and that's where the extra value lies.

4 **Don't discount, reduce.** Have you ever seen salespeople who offer thousands of pounds worth of services for just £500? What this tells me is that those services aren't worth very much to discount them so drastically. People will always negotiate, and they want to walk away thinking they have got a good deal. But when it comes to pricing, the customer isn't always right. You have spent time building your business, knowledge and experience and these aren't negotiable. And as soon as you discount your prices, you are instantly telling the customer that your services aren't worth what you're asking. So instead, offer a reduced service, or remove features that they have previously requested. This will either make them buy into the full service or give you opportunities to upsell in the future. And you haven't negotiated your worth.

5 **Add it all up.** Your incomings need to cover your outgoings, from overheads, to time and resources, labour and additional costs, and this all needs to be wrapped up in your pricing. By calculating these spends, and then adding profit on top, you'll be able to work out what pricing structure is best, and most effective for you, whether it be hourly rate, retainer or project based.

Don't be afraid to say no. Not everyone is right for you and your business, and it is never worth sticking it out with anyone who doesn't appreciate your worth, or level of service. One no can save several months of stress.

Product-based business

A product-based business is one where you create products and sell them to customers for them to use themselves. Unlike a service-based business, where you are selling a trade or skill, a product-based business holds physical stock. This means there are big questions about how you are going to create, manufacture, distribute and market your product, but less focus on clients, pricing (as it's somewhat dictated by the market rate) and growing a team.

Of course, there is more of an overlap nowadays with the boom in digital, as many of you may also create a digital product – such as an e-book, online course, workshop or training – where a financial transaction takes place to buy a product, but it's delivered electronically. These kinds of physical products can be a great income boost for any business, allowing them to increase revenue without having to hire additional staff.

Traditional product-based businesses rely on research and development to create a product, but once launched, the growth can be exponential without increasing overheads drastically – you can sell one product a thousand times. Thus, product-based companies can be easier to scale and grow quickly.

Examples of product-based businesses include:

- food or drink product;
- beauty product;
- wellness product;
- technology business;
- mobile app;
- clothing and fashion;
- stationery, homeware or interiors.

Pros of product-based businesses

There are many considerations to make before launching a product-based business. Here are a few of the benefits as I see it:

- **Extensibility** – business growth in a product-based business relies on developing products and selling them. This means your business doesn't necessarily need a larger number of employees or a bigger office to grow. You can **scale** with a limited number of employees.

↪ More **growth potential** – your growth is not dependent on how many hours you can work, but how many people will buy your products. By that very nature, there's huge potential in a product business to grow.

↪ **Innovation!** – product-based businesses can be great fun; you're in control of designing the product, creating the visions and values for the business and driving creativity. You're not at the behest of your client's desires and have total freedom to create a business on your terms.

↪ **Outsourcing** – once the product has been designed, much of the manufacturing and distribution can be outsourced, freeing up time for you to continue to innovate, market and grow your business.

↪ **Economies of scale** – the more your business grows in sales, the lower you'll be able to get your costs down because manufacturers will often give more favourable terms to larger orders. This provides huge potential as your business grows!

↪ **Structured revenue** – there's an element of service-based businesses which will always be unstable: you're relying on a healthy pipeline of new clients, keeping existing ones and enough supply for the demand. But with product-based businesses, continuous revenue is easier to achieve. With the help of a great marketing and sales team, you can project your cash flow and sales based on previous months and have a good grip on the pipeline.

Cons of product-based businesses

That said, whilst the growth and scale can be tempting, there are some downsides to product-based businesses, as outlined below:

↪ There's more **risk** involved – not only will you have to invest time and energy into your business before launch, there's also considerable financial costs involved. You need to spend money on developing the idea and at least a prototype of a product, plus all the legal costs involved, such as trademarking.

↳ Unknown **demand** – you can research the product but there's always a risk that people may not buy the product. It's a gamble, and whilst you can minimize that risk through market research, there's always an element of uncertainty in a product business.

↳ Requires **upfront investment** – you're going to need to put in more money with a product business, so you may look for investors or take out a bank loan. Either way, there's more financial pressure from the start with a product business.

↳ **Customer service, marketing and PR** – it's crucial to keep good relationships with your customers and a buzz around your product, so you'll need to invest in great customer service, marketing and PR. Customer service can be time-consuming – don't overlook the dedication it takes to keep this up.

WORKBOOK

Q1: Which kind of business appeals to you more – product- or service-based?

_____

_____

_____

Q2: What aspects of each model appeal to you and why?

_____

_____

_____

Q3: What skills do you think complement this business type? What are your strengths and weaknesses that need to be identified to move to the next level?

_____

_____

_____

_____

_____

Q4: Who are going to be your 'accountability' partners on this
journey?

_____

_____

_____

Q5: What are the next steps you need to take to turn your idea into
a reality? List three. When do you wish to complete these by?

_____

_____

_____

_____

CASE STUDY   She Made It: Steph Douglas

Name: Steph Douglas
Job title: CEO and founder of Don't Buy Her Flowers

What was the inspiration behind launching your company?

When I had my first baby I was inundated with beautiful, well-meant
bouquets; as I sat feeling overwhelmed, exhausted and emotional, it
struck me as a bizarre gift – to give someone another thing to look after
when they're doing more caring than they've ever done in their life.
When I spoke with friends having babies around the same time, they all
said the same – they'd received lots of flowers and it was clear there
could be better gifts that offer some TLC.

What problem were you trying to solve with the business?

Initially it was gift packages for new mums that were all about
encouraging her to take a bit of time for herself. I recognized that new

mums were often overwhelmed, unsure of themselves, tired and all at a time when you might be hearing that you should be 'savouring every moment'. If I'm honest, I underestimated quite how powerful that was – the idea of someone recognizing you might be feeling those things and sending a gift that was all about *you*. There's a real human connection which you don't get with all gifts – we immediately had customers saying their recipient had cried when they opened it, and then people saying they wanted to send packages for birthdays and get well and suddenly it's a much bigger market than what I was launching with.

What inspires you daily to keep growing and building the business?

I feel massive responsibility to my team, to ensure it continues to grow so I can continue not only paying them but offering them opportunities and a brilliant place to work. Building a brand and a culture I'm proud of has become a huge part of the job. I also can see the potential with DBHF – I think we're just hitting our stride and it's getting really exciting.

What advice would you give women looking to launch their own business?

It pains me to say it, but the reality is that *most* women, especially if they have a family, still do the majority at home. It's changing but we're not there yet. So I see a lot of women starting a business but still trying to juggle all that they did before and it's just not possible. It might take some big conversations with a partner, accepting help, lowering standards, all of the above. To give yourself the best start to focus and put energy into a business, you're going to have to take something out and clear some space. Men have been doing it forever.

How do you know you're starting the right business for you?

I don't think you ever do – I think the idea of a business for life is misleading and we probably shouldn't be afraid to do something for a few years and then move on to something else. But obviously when you start you need passion, the right skills, to be the best ambassador for whatever it is you do. And work out what success looks like for you and keep checking back to it. It's different for everyone.

What makes your business stand out in a crowded marketplace?

Our gifts are very much about thoughtfulness, from the products we select to the recyclable packaging to our super-serving customer services and personal touches like the handwritten tag. We have grown considerably, but the core idea remains – to offer TLC, to make someone feel loved. The team really care – they're in it with me and that comes through in everything we do.

How did you finance the business at the start? Did you raise investment?

We've self-funded the business. That's meant keeping overheads low to start – I ran the business from my house for the first two years, initially doing everything from packing orders and stock management to customer services. I didn't take a salary and didn't have a marketing budget so had a blog and used social media and PR to get DBHF out there. Every time we started to make money, we've reinvested it – in people or new premises. We've just experienced huge growth since the start of COVID-19, which is a bizarre position to be in and I know how fortunate we've been when so many people are facing a really tough time. We now want to maintain that position.

Any advice on getting the business model right from the start?

I think stay focused – you don't need to launch with your final offering or product. You need to strip it back and start with getting what you do 'do' right, learning from your customers, and then taking them with you as you grow and have more to offer. No one has ever launched with their final product. There are so many different options when it comes to finance, so it has to be what works for you. For everything, try not to be influenced by what you think everyone else is doing.

Is there a secret to growth or is it just about hard work?

That first couple of years takes a lot of work – getting something off the ground is hard work – maximizing opportunities and staying focused. But I also recognize there's luck and timing involved. The growth in awareness of mental health and that idea of reaching out to others, the fact we've been able to set up a warehouse in Gloucestershire headed up by my brother, which is considerably more cost-efficient than a space in London where I live. I've certainly never worked harder, but it feels very different when it's your own thing.

CHAPTER TEN

How to structure and finance your business

Now you've got a clear idea of the kind of business type you'd like to run, let's go deeper into the practical considerations of starting your own business.

The process of launching a business can be intimidating. This chapter will guide you through all the larger things to consider pre-launch and how to set yourself up for success. There are some big decisions to make on how you structure your business and the kind of long-term plan you put in place to guide it.

Let's first look at practical steps that every aspiring entrepreneur can take to get started.

Nine steps to starting your business

Whether it's a service or product business, there are a few crucial steps you must take to get your business off the ground.

Step one: identify your target market

Once you've developed your business idea, spend some time thinking about your target audience. You can even sketch out your ideal customer on paper, giving them a face, name and identity – I find this really helps the idea come to life. Grab a pen and answer these questions:

↳ What age, background and income are my target customers?
↳ Where are my audience spending time? Where do they shop? What are their spending habits?
↳ Do they need my product/service?
↳ Why would they choose my business over my competitors?

Step two: understand the problem you're solving

Every business should be solving some kind of problem, and their service or product is meeting a need. We'll be delving deeper into this topic in Chapter 12, but, for now, make sure *you* know what you're trying to achieve with your business offering – this is like the compass that will direct and guide you. Here are a few questions to consider:

↳ Do I know what problem I am trying to solve with my business?
↳ Have other companies tried to do this in the past? How can I improve on this offering?
↳ How big an issue is this problem?
↳ How can I make my offering more unique and special?
↳ Am I trying to change the behaviour and habits of my customers?
↳ Is this a problem my customer faces daily/weekly/yearly?
↳ How am I going to communicate my unique offering?

Step three: write a business plan

A business plan is a blueprint that will guide you from launching as a startup, to the growth and hiring phase. It's tempting to rush in when you've got a new business idea, but by slowing down and putting a plan in place for your business, you'll be giving yourself a clear roadmap for success.

Every business is different, and the detail of your plan is largely guided by how much external support you need. For example, if you're trying to raise investment and need capital to get off the ground, you may need a very detailed and comprehensive business plan. If you plan to launch as a solopreneur with your own cash, the business plan is largely for yourself. Below is a guide to different business plans and how to get started writing them:

TOP TIPS: WRITING A TRADITIONAL BUSINESS PLAN

If you're looking to get financial support from an institution or investor, you'll need a detailed business plan that provides all the necessary information on your concept. Here's what you need to include:

Executive summary

This is the first section of your business plan, which is a key, concise statement about your business. The brief summary should include: your business name, the problem it solves, the target market and your mission statement. You may find writing this last is helpful once you've established more information for yourself. A mission statement is not something that can be rushed, and it may take time to discover the true purpose and vision of your company.

Company description

This second section outlines all the important details of the company and gives potential investors a sense of who you are as a

---

leader, what you wish to achieve and your drive for the future. All crucial information should be included in this, such as:

- location;
- size of the company;
- what your company does;
- what you wish to accomplish;
- your vision and direction of the company.

Products and services

You need to make your offering clear to any potential investor. The products and services part of your business plan should outline what you're selling, to whom, and the clear value you're bringing to customers or clients with your business. It would also be worth noting any pricing, similar companies in the field and plans for future offerings.

Market analysis

Showing an awareness and understanding of the industry you're launching into is crucial for investors. This section is your opportunity to do just that. You should provide a detailed overview of the industry in which you plan to operate, including any statistics to support your claims. You may also want to discuss your target market and competition.

Marketing plan

Once you've outlined your chosen market, demonstrate how you plan to attract them. You should include your planned pricing, promotions and how you're going to sell your product and service, especially any digital marketing channels you may use.

Management summary

A management summary is essentially an overview of how the business is structured – this would include any details pertinent to the company's structure, including:

- business structure, for example private limited company (Ltd), limited liability company (LLC) or partnership;

- the management team, such as a board of directors;
- planned management hires – who you wish to hire and what their role will be;
- external support you may need, ie accountants, bookkeeping, public relations;
- growth plan, such as how many people you wish to hire in the next few years and what their salaries would be.

Financial analysis

This is a crucial part of the business plan. It contains all the important numbers for your business that investors would wish to see. The financial overview should include:

- the current finances of your business, such as turnover and profit from the last financial year;
- investment needed for growth, ie how much money you need now and why;
- estimated costs involved in growing, for example operating expenses and payroll;
- a projection for gross revenue over the coming years – setting financial goals and targets.

Appendices and supporting information

You can end your business plan with any additional information that supports your proposal, including charts, graphs, statistics or any research you've undertaken. Anything that can support your offering with information to back it up will be great in front of investors.

TOP TIPS: WRITING A SIMPLE ONE-PAGE BUSINESS PLAN

If you're not looking to raise investment for your business, you may wish to write a simpler business plan that's for your own use. The business plan will vary on whether you're planning a service- or product-based business, and you may want to research further on how to write business plans for these two different types.

A great book on this is *How to Write a Business Plan* by Brian Fitch, published by Kogan Page.

It's a really great idea to have a business plan in any situation, as it's something to guide you – remember it's a living document, so it's always evolving and can change as your business grows. Here's what you might like to include on a one-page business plan:

Vision

The first section should cover your dreams and vision for the business and what you're trying to achieve with it. Write down any important details to do with the vision, such as whether you wish to sell it in the future and what kind of growth you're looking for.

Service-based business questions

↪ Where do you see the business in five years?

↪ How do you plan to grow?

↪ How do you plan to hire?

↪ What is the vision for the business you're building?

Product-based business questions

↪ What is your dream for this business?

↪ How big do you see the business getting?

↪ How do you plan to grow the business and who are the key hires to make this happen?

↪ Do you plan to sell the business in time?

Mission statement

This is an overview of the mission of the business – explain what product/service you're offering and why. This goes into the finer details of your business vision, including any practical elements such as target market.

Service-based business questions

↪ Who is your dream client/customer?

↪ What services are you offering to them?

↪ What is your unique selling proposition, ie how will your offering address the needs of your customer?

↪ How will you provide the service: will it be remotely, in person or through a third party?

Product-based business questions

↪ What is your target market?

↪ What products are you selling?

↪ How are these product offerings different from competitors?

↪ How will you sell your products – online or physically?

↪ How will you manufacture your products?

↪ How will you deliver your products?

Pricing

This section should make it clear how your business is going to become profitable.

Service-based business questions

↪ How much will you charge for your services?

↪ How will you make your pricing attractive yet profitable?

Product-based business questions

↪ How much will your products cost?

↪ How does this compare with other products on the market?

Advertising and marketing

Include a brief outline of your marketing and advertising plan for your business, including any channels you think will be crucial to your growth.

Service-based business questions

↪ How are you going to market your services?

↪ Which channels are you going to use the most?

↪ Are you going to produce any marketing materials?

↳ How are you going to attract new clients?

↳ What will the branding look like?

Product-based business questions

↳ How are you going to market your products?

↳ Will you use any sales promotions?

↳ What channels will you focus on for marketing?

↳ Will you put paid spend behind marketing your products?

↳ How will you engage with customer feedback?

Objectives

Service-based business questions

↳ What are the main objectives for your business?

↳ What business targets would you like to hit?

↳ What changes in the business objectives are you planning for, for example seasonality?

Product-based business questions

↳ What metrics are you using for success, ie how many products do you wish to sell?

↳ What are the biggest challenges of reaching those objectives?

Action steps

Briefly describe the action steps you need to take to make your vision a reality.

Service-based business questions

↳ What are your next action steps?

↳ What are the highest priority steps for you right now?

Product-based business questions

↳ What are your next steps?

↳ When do you wish to take this action by?

As you can now see, a business plan is a great way to give you structure, direction and focus for the future, so whether it's for yourself or an investor, it's a valuable use of your time and energy. Even the most complex and ambitious businesses can have a simple one-page business plan, so try not to overcomplicate things for yourself!

Step four: get a grip on your finances

One of the reasons I was compelled to write this book is that I find many business books either focus *too* heavily on the self-help side of being an entrepreneur (mindset, positivity, self-belief) or *too* heavily on the practical and financial considerations of running a business, but both are equally important.

You need to believe you have all the tools inside you to be a successful founder and commit wholeheartedly to your business vision. At the same time, if you don't have an understanding of cash flow, revenue structure and investment, you can manifest all you want, but it won't help you.

So perhaps the most important step is getting intimate with the finances of the business and projections for the future. Again, some of the finer details will depend on whether it's a service or product business – and as we've looked at, service businesses often need less startup capital – but a general understanding of where cash is coming in and out in your business is key.

In general, I think we tend to overcomplicate the relationship with money in a business. Sometimes you need to simplify the issue for yourself with these basic questions:

↳ How much money do I need to start the business?
↳ How will I get that money?
↳ How do I plan to make money with my business?
↳ How much money do I think I can make in year one, two and five?

↳ How long will it take me to start making *profit* in the business?

↳ How much of a cash reserve/buffer do I need, just in case?

↳ How much do I need to spend to make the business start making profit?

↳ What will my overheads be?

↳ Will my overhead increase as I grow?

For the first question, you may find that you need a financial injection to get things started. If so, there are a variety of investment options available to you, which I've outlined below:

Funding your business: the options

The best thing to do is start a business with minimal upfront investment. It gives you freedom, flexibility and less pressure, as well as being able to retain more of the business. If you go for investment early, you *may* have already given away a slice of equity (the value of the shares in your company) – and you could undervalue your business at the start because you're not really sure what it's worth yet.

That said, it's not always possible to start a business without a cash injection. If you need capital up front, there are a variety of routes available to fund your business.

FRIENDS AND FAMILY

Raising money from your personal network can be one way of funding your business. This can be a simple way to raise money with set repayment terms, but of course the downside is that it can put a strain on your personal relationships and cause additional pressure. If you choose this route, try not to make it too informal. You should still have an agreement in place that clearly lays out the terms of the arrangement.

CROWDFUNDING

Crowdfunding is where you fund a project by raising relatively small amounts of money from a large number of people through the internet. The most popular platforms for crowdfunding are Kickstarter, Indiegogo, Crowdfunder and Angel List. Research the best crowdfunding platform for you. Each will vary in what you have to give away in return for investment, such as equity, product or rewards. Launching a successful crowdfunding campaign takes planning – you need to hone the brand message, vision and purpose, and incentivize people to invest by translating your passion for the business.

ANGEL INVESTMENT

Angel investing is the most significant source of investment in startups seeking equity to grow their business. Angel investing is where a high-net-worth individual makes use of their personal disposable finance to invest in a business. They can invest alone or as part of a group of angels. An angel will often seek a return on their investment within a period of three to eight years, so they will be looking to see if your business can meet certain criteria from the get-go. Wondering where to look to find angels? The UK Angel Investment Network is a great resource with lots of angels listed publicly.

VENTURE CAPITAL

Venture capital is another form of private equity financing, through managed funds, which are raised with private or public money. The venture capital manager will invest money on behalf of the fund. VCs tend to be more risk-averse and are less likely to invest small amounts in the startup or early-stage period. Business angels often take a different approach from venture capital, with 'patient capital', where they are less concerned about the rapid return of their investment and happy to support the business through its path to growth.

BUSINESS INCUBATORS AND ACCELERATORS

Another increasingly popular option for startups is to join an incubator or accelerator. An incubator 'incubates' disruptive ideas, with the hope of building a business model and company out of it – often individuals will join an incubator without a clear business in mind. An accelerator, on the other hand, focuses on helping an existing business scale and grow – this might mean giving the founders new tools and training to help supercharge their business. On both occasions, pay close attention to the legal implications of joining one of these programmes, as they will often ask for equity in the business in return for support.

BANK LOAN

Getting a bank loan for your business is perhaps one of the most straightforward ways of raising finance if you don't want to give away any equity. Many banks will offer flexible borrowing for your business – meaning that interest rates are fixed and you can choose the terms – with loans of up to £100,000. Many banks will also offer a six-month repayment holiday at the start of your loan, giving you some time to get the business off the ground and start generating revenue.

GOVERNMENT SCHEMES

It's always worth checking what government-backed schemes are available in your locality. Many governments will provide benefits, including tax relief, to entrepreneurs and create startup initiatives to encourage innovation. For women in particular, there's a focus in the UK of encouraging more women to excel in tech and stem. If your business is in a particularly male-dominated industry, there may be special grants available to you.

WHAT INVESTORS ARE LOOKING FOR

Emilia Gyoerk is an investor and alumni at the Startup Leadership Program London. Building on seven years in financial services at the European Central Bank and Moody's Investors Service, she is now the investment manager at Future Flow Group, which invests in early-stage tech-driven startups.

She has supported over a dozen startups across finance, advertising, VR, digital consumer products, and SaaS solution. Here Emilia shares her top tips for what investors are looking for in early-stage investments:

↳ **Digital:** regardless of the product you're creating, you must have a robust digital infrastructure and delivery. Now, more than ever, it's not just the digital presence, but also the digital readiness of a business that is crucial. The ongoing digital transformation of the economy requires that services can be delivered on demand digitally, at the comfort and convenience of the customer, be it a business or an individual.

↳ **Flexibility:** a business needs to be able to adapt and re-adapt to unforeseen risks and market developments in a rapidly changing global economy. The market is unforgiving to businesses that are slow or unable to adapt. A clear example of this has been the COVID-19 outbreak, which has left businesses unable to adapt or withstand the economic pressure to fail, while survivors emerge more resilient than ever.

↳ **Scalability:** for a business to be investable it needs to be scalable and target a very large market. Investors will reward a business that has a large addressable market ahead of a business that targets a concentrated niche at a small scale.

↳ **Connections:** an entrepreneur who can leverage her network has higher chances to succeed, therefore also a higher chance of attracting investment. Such connections are often derived from founders' participation in entrepreneurial development programmes. It's important for founders to learn vital practical skills about entrepreneurship, while building their networks. This can lead to support in marketing, fundraising, new employees, or introductions to other stakeholders and partners.

CASE STUDY   She Made It: Hilary Rowland

Name: Hilary Rowland

Job title: Co-founder and creative director of BOOM Cycle

How did the idea for your business come about?

When I first moved to London, spinning was only in gyms and it was not consistently good. My husband and I started the business together – we were the first to market for dedicated spin studios on a large scale in England.

What steps did you take to launch?

For our first studio, we did (rather limited) market research, wrote a business plan and took out a bank loan and personal investment commitment. From there, we identified the perfect site, did a fundraise, fit-out and launched.

How did you finance the business?

We sold a house and got a bank loan, then approached angel investors for the rest. We have now been through many more rounds of fundraising to get to where we are today.

Any advice for fundraising for startups? What mistakes did you make with raising money?

The main thing is to make sure you're at the right stage for investment, then target your business to those companies that fund your stage and fund your sector. You'll end up kissing a lot of frogs so don't be disheartened by lots of people saying no. The other thing is it'll always take longer than you think, so start early and spend as much time prepping as possible.

How do you manage cash flow as a business? Any tips for better money management?

Make sure you have data fast and set parameters for variable costs which need to move with revenues. For example, we'll set different staffing levels at a percentage of revenue, but it's no use giving a parameter and finding out six weeks later it's way off. We'll keep an eye on that weekly and make adjustments immediately. There are great products like Float that'll link in with accounting software and have made cash flow forecasting so much easier for the untrained person.

What's been the biggest learning curve as an entrepreneur?

Try and see the big picture as much as possible! It's easy to get sucked into the ups and downs on a daily basis, but if you're always rising and falling you get exhausted quicker and frustration can set in.

Step five: choose your business identity

The next step on the business launch plan is getting the company's name, identity and branding in place. When it comes to choosing a business name, there are a few things to consider:

↪ Avoid anything hard to spell.
↪ Make sure the domain and all the social media accounts are available.
↪ Don't pick a name that's too niche or narrowing, in case your business concept changes.
↪ Check the trademark and search engine optimization (SEO) on the name.
↪ Use a name that conveys meaning, and people can easily 'get'.
↪ Get feedback from others on the name.
↪ Make sure the name sounds good when said aloud!

Branding is something that's crucial for your business's success, but it can't be rushed and may need several iterations to get right.

TOP TIPS: HOW TO TAKE YOUR BRAND FROM IDEA TO VISUALIZATION

Lucy Hitchcock is the founder of Sassy Digital, a no-nonsense branding, marketing and web designer for businesses. Below Lucy shares her top tips on creating visual imagery that supports your brand and values. She thinks there are some steps for product-based businesses which act as a launch pad into design:

1 **Who are you appealing to? What are your customers' aspirations and what aesthetics appeal to them?** Once you have an idea of your audience, you'll have a better sense of the brand identity that would appeal to them. For example, are you creating a product that would be great to share on Instagram? That's an important consideration for the unboxing experience.

2 **Create a mood board** – we use Pinterest boards for all our clients, which have different sections with colours, fonts, styles and ideas. Also, consider brand photography. What kind of photography do you think your brand will use on their marketing and social media? Your logo can't mismatch what your visuals are going to be.

3 **Once we've done that, we can start to produce a brand.** Mock up how the branding looks on a variety of formats – such as labels, swing tags, social media, websites – to see it in situ and make sure that it's right for your brand.

4 **You don't build a brand by changing it a year in.** You want to start right. Check you're happy with the branding the first time around. Your branding should be able to stand the test of time so that people recognize your branding for years to come. It's much harder to do a redesign once you've got established customers.

5 **Create a brand guidelines document.** Think about fonts, colours and how your logo will be used as part of a wider picture. Remember, building a brand is about taking how you look (branding) and how you sound (writing and talking) to help your customers feel a certain way. A brand guidelines document will help you ensure the way your brand looks stays consistent no matter who helps you develop the way you look in the future.

6 **What do you need to complement your brand?** For example, do you need packaging slips that stand out? What's going to help your brand go viral? One thing I think about a lot is that unboxing experience from a customer's point of view. How can brand collateral make your customers feel excited?

7 **How can you make the branding more personal?** Perhaps you can add a hand-written or script element to your branding, so it feels more personal.

8 **Use creative copy for your brand.** Phrases like 'we hope you love this product as much as we do!' are totally overused. Don't go half-hearted with the brand copy – be bold and do something different!

Step six: sort out legals, trademarks and licences

This will of course vary depending on the industry, but make sure to research any licences you may need for your business to operate. For example, if it's a street food business, you'll need a specific licence for food hygiene and safety. If you're starting a service-based business, contracts are key and it's really worth investing in an inexpensive solicitor who will draw up a template that you can use for clients. Contracts are there to protect both you and your client, and both parties benefit from having a clear agreement in place.

Step seven: accounting and book-keeping

Accounting! Boring but important. Having a great accountant is crucial. You want someone you can grow with, who understands the challenges and demands of your business. Lots of accounting firms will give favourable rates to startups, but you need someone to support you, who understands the financial implications of different business models and can help with your tax return. A book-keeper who helps manage your weekly expenses and keeps a log of outgoings may also be useful. Otherwise, accounting software such as QuickBooks and Xero can serve you well in the early days.

Step eight: hiring a team

Once you've got the majority of your business plan and finances in place, you may think about bringing on a team member to help support you. There's no wrong or right time to hire someone – and hey, hiring might not even be your goal – but I think there are a few warning signs that you need additional support. These include: feeling like your workload is ever-mounting and you can't get through it; feeling 'out of your depth' with certain areas of your business; or feeling like you've reached a ceiling with what you're able to achieve single-handedly right now.

The first hire is tricky. You want someone that's going to help expand the business and its mission, but first hires are often where the mistakes are made, because you're not really sure what you're looking for – or the business is in a 'messy' startup stage. Here are a few tips I can share on your first hire:

↳ Hire for culture, train for skill. It's wonderful if you can find someone who does both, but in my personal experience, it's easier to train someone who might be under-qualified for the job but has the right energy, passion and attitude than to make someone 'fit' with your working culture who already has all the training.

↳ Find someone with an entrepreneurial spirit. This will really help you find someone who fits into the pace and working environment of the business.

↳ Don't overlook instinct. Sometimes we just get a 'feel' for a person very quickly. Those gut reactions are important. Don't ignore any feelings you may have with a potential employee.

↳ Hire in a way that your business can afford. Don't commit to spending more money than you have – this may mean bringing someone on part-time or on a freelance basis. This can be a great way to expand the work of your company in a way that's financially flexible to you – and with the move towards self-employed and working from home, you may find lots of people that are looking for work in a non-traditional setup.

Step nine: create a marketing plan

We're going to delve deep into marketing your business later, but for now, just know that a marketing plan *is* very important, and you shouldn't be tempted to rush launching without one in place – no matter how excited you are about your business!

Understanding who your customer is, where they hang out online and how to speak to them in a way that converts into sales is the foundation of any good marketing plan.

WORKBOOK

Q1: What have you learned in this chapter about the steps you need to take to launch your business?

_____

_____

_____

_____

Q2: What part of the nine-step plan intimidates you the most and why?

_____

_____

_____

_____

Q3: What can you do to help support yourself at this time? Where does more learning need to happen?

_____

_____

_____

_____

Q4: How do you feel about the business plan you've written? What did you find hardest about it?

_____

_____

_____

_____

Q5: Who would be your first hire and why? What additional support would you like from a team member?

_____

_____

_____

_____

CASE STUDY   She Made It: Rachel Carrell

Name: Rachel Carrell
Job title: Founder and CEO of Koru Kids

How did the idea for Koru Kids come about?

When I had a baby, I experienced how frustrating childcare can be first-hand. I learned how expensive it was and it was almost impossible to find any that was good quality.

I got really fed up about this and thought, 'I'll join a company to help with this problem,' and was gobsmacked to find there was little out there. Coming from the world of health tech, which is full of startups, specialist venture capitalists and investment funds, there was virtually nothing. So: I decided to do it myself and founded Koru Kids.

What do you think are the biggest barriers facing women in the workplace today?

The COVID-19 pandemic exposed a lot of gender inequality. There's clear evidence now that women do the majority of the childcare responsibilities during the pandemic, which is a huge issue for women in the workplace.

There are some positives out of the pandemic too – parents are finding it amazing having their children around all the time, and there's also evidence that fathers are getting more involved with their children's lives and education than ever before, which is fantastic.

It's impossible to devote all your mind to working and look after small children at the same time. The lack of affordable and reliable childcare – that is easy to find – is a huge barrier to women in the workplace.

What more needs to be done to help support working mothers in the UK?

Childcare needs to be flexible; it needs to support part-time working and working non-traditional hours.

The childcare system is set up premised on an assumption that you work full-time in an office from 9–5. None of those things are true anymore.

Many people want to work around the school run, or in the evening and spend some time with their kids during the day. We need to be more flexible in our approach.

Also, a huge percentage of women want to work part-time and, unfortunately, lots of childcare expect parents to work full-time. This means part-time care is much more expensive and difficult to find.

How can you be a compassionate but strong leader?

I don't think these two things are at all in opposition. There's strength in compassion and there are times where you have to remind yourself to be compassionate.

Sometimes, you have to exercise self-discipline because something that's happened may have triggered something in you. You may be a little focused on yourself in the moment and you may have to remind yourself to be compassionate.

What can companies do to attract more women to work in their businesses?

I think it's about the importance of meritocracy and building a company where you're rewarded for the work that you do and not for what you appear to be doing.

It's important to have your recognition and reward structure set up so that the quiet person who comes in every day, does a wonderful job, never blows their own trumpet, and just diligently gets on with it, is equally rewarded as the person who thinks a lot about how they're externally perceived and positions themselves.

Whilst that's not always a gender thing, I've observed that men are better at the kind of political positioning and often women are the ones who come in and just do a great job, but don't necessarily get the recognition for it.

What was your experience of raising investment like, especially as a woman?

I was not only raising as a woman but also for a very female business: childcare. I think it's important to go into these things with a positive mindset – if you're looking for things like micro-aggressions, it's not the right headspace to be in.

The single biggest thing for me is that I had a baby in the middle of my second fund-raise. I raised £3.5 million and I had a baby at the same time – literally. I had the baby on the Sunday and went back to work the next day. I was doing in-person meetings on the Wednesday. When you are really committed to your vision and purpose, you don't even think about it.

CHAPTER ELEVEN

Problem-solving businesses

In this chapter, we're going to be looking at how you can make your business solution-focused and serve the needs of your consumer. So often, with business, we think in terms of what *we* want to build – our personal dream business and revenue – and we can overlook the real needs of our audience. Creating a successful business is about understanding what problem you're solving and then establishing an offering which is better than the company who has come before – finding ways to innovate in a space that brings something fresh and new.

Be careful not to be too fixed in your mindset on what you want your business to be – you'll learn that by being compassionate and listening to your audience, your business can go on an unexpected journey based on what's working and gaining the most momentum. The key with any business that is trying to solve a problem or meet a particular need is to listen really diligently to your audience – create spaces where you can gather feedback, interact with them (ideally in a physical sense, not just on social media!) and grow together.

Often, with business, we like to *think* we're in control. We're the ones who have created something. We're looking to commercialize their need – and ultimately make money. But, in fact, our consumer is always the one in control – without them, there is no business. So be careful not to try to force something on your consumer – look at ways to interact and engage with them in a way that allows your business concept to continually thrive.

In this chapter, we're going to be looking at what problem you're trying to solve with your business and how to use your unique voice to communicate that solution-based offering. You may find through this work that your business offering isn't crystal clear enough yet on what it's trying to achieve for the consumer and why. And, hey, that's okay.

Creating a successful solution-focused business takes time – and you may find that it takes several iterations of your business to make an authentic connection between your consumer and the bigger picture. Be gentle and compassionate with yourself on this journey too – sometimes it's the things that don't work which lead us to the successful projects.

Let's dive in!

Problem-solving business: seven steps to success

As a brief overview, these are the fundamentals of building a business that has problem-solving at its core:

1 Define the problem.
2 Do the right research.
3 Get to the root of the problem.
4 Be open-minded with the solution.
5 Prioritize efficacy.
6 Be a problem-solving leader.
7 Communicate your message.

Let's now look a little deeper at each of those and look at some potential hurdles you might face.

1. Define the problem

Clarity, clarity, clarity. Often, we want to find a solution to a problem before we even really know what it is. Sometimes, we really want to be 'useful' with our businesses and we can end up blowing the whole problem out of proportion. Be careful of trying to jump into a solution before you really know the problem intimately – getting clarity on a problem means understanding the heart of the issue and how your business benefits its customers.

Here are a few top tips on defining the problem:

↪ Make sure to separate fact from opinion and speculation.
↪ Work out the underlying causes that are creating this problem.
↪ Explicitly state the problem – to yourself and others.
↪ Avoid stating the problem as a disguised solution.

What is a problem anyway?

I think it's important to make a distinction between what is a problem and what is a fact of life. Some things exist and don't actually need to be changed; others are genuine problems that are frustrating and we face daily. Understanding the scale and size of the problem is important – how many people does this affect? How serious is the problem? How much does it actually bug people?

2. Do the right research

When doing research, try to speak to people outside of your immediate circle – I find we can often get caught up in our own social and economic milieu, and if you're only asking like-minded people from a similar background about this problem, chances are you're not getting an accurate read on things!

Do research that covers a wide net of experiences and backgrounds, so you can understand the problem you're solving from different angles.

3. Get to the root of the problem

Be careful of treating the symptom of a problem rather than the root cause; get to the heart of the problem by understanding *why* it's happening, not just how it's manifesting in everyday life. If you're only solving a symptom of the problem with your business, you'll end up trying to re-solve the same problem further down the line again.

4. Be open-minded with the solution

You may have identified a problem through your business and think you have the solution, but it's important to look at all possible solutions. The more possible solutions you come up with, the more chance you'll end up with the right one.

5. Prioritize efficacy

There may be several routes you can take to solving this particular problem, but, when in doubt, always prioritize the one that requires the least upfront capital, minimum time to launch and can provide the quickest solution. A solution that is higher in complexity and cost and has a longer timeframe may be a more enticing option, but if it makes a difference between doing it or not, then go for the quicker option!

EXERCISE: UNDERSTANDING YOUR OFFERING

Get a pen and paper and spend some time answering these questions:

What problem am I trying to solve with my business?

Is this problem personal to me? What's my experience of it?

What have companies done previously to solve this problem?

How can I improve and build upon that offering?

What is my company going to do differently?

How am I going to communicate my offering to my audience?

What channels will best support communicating this offering?

CASE STUDY   She Made It: Christina Taylor

Name: Christina Taylor
Job title: Founder of Aim Sky High

How did the idea for your company come about?

Aim Sky High developed through community work that I started when I was 13 years old. I started my own dance group in a local youth centre. Aged 16 it had grown to 23 girls the same age as me. We were all from disadvantaged backgrounds so I always had to apply for funding and fundraise to enable us to access opportunities. From the age of 16–19 I received over £70,000 worth of funding to run community dance projects. I then started teaching younger children. Whilst at university studying business and politics, the government defunded all our local youth centres so I either had to stop the activities that were engaging so many disenfranchised youth with no opportunities, or find a way to make it work. Aim Sky High was the solution to a problem I cared so deeply about I wanted to solve.

How did you go about getting it off the ground?

I sought advice all the time. Luckily for me, I had already had a structure in place and a small customer base. However, my university lecturers helped, I engaged in a lot of research, and the top and bottom of it is, I was just brave enough to give it a go. You can sit and research and come up with ideas to your heart's content, but you never really get full lowdown until you throw yourself in. Although the research helped, I had many hurdles to overcome!

Do you have any advice for aspiring female entrepreneurs?

Always educate yourself – you can never know too much. Be persistent and reach out to people. Create your own space and build your own doors to open; do not ever be disheartened by a no. For aspiring female entrepreneurs with children, please remember children follow actions more than they do words: if you want them to be brave and tenacious, show them. Connect with other female entrepreneurs: we often share different struggles from our male counterparts, and having a network you can call upon and vent is everything.

Failure is not a bad thing – it means you are getting closer to the win; don't be disheartened. Even if you are not confident in your ability at the moment, have the confidence to try.

What does 'purpose' in work mean to you?

Purpose in work means to do something that creates positive change in a way that fulfils you. Different people feel a sense of affinity to different causes, therefore everybody's individual purpose will be different, but we can all create positive change and affect society in some way, shape or form that makes us feel fulfilled. There is no pressure to find that – many people take years. There is no guilt in not knowing, but it is something worth exploring because your work will feel so much more joyful.

How can you connect with your deeper purpose with work?

I believe you can connect with your deeper purpose with work by figuring out what you really care about and what cause and issue triggers you to action. You can then either go into work in that field or use a field as a tool to aid the long-term mission. For example, I use dance and the performing arts to address social mobility as opposed to directly working in social mobility research.

Also, I think it is important to be engaged in your work. If you are doing something you really do not enjoy, the likelihood is that you will not want to go over and above and it is harder to create a positive work environment. A positive work environment typically stimulates ideas, energy and collaboration with other great minds. Therefore, going into a field or job that you enjoy is important as it will lead to other opportunities and you are more inspired to continue learning.

How can you create a business that does good?

First of all, a business is a vehicle that is meant to provide a solution to a problem. Therefore, finding a problem that changes people's lives for the better is a good start. A company like Amazon creates convenience and time saving for customers, which changes people's lives for the better, hence why it is so successful, but it does not provide the same social value as a venture that aims to solve social issues.

However, a business that does good goes beyond the problem it solves. It has to stand with integrity and morals throughout every inch of the company. For instance, the supply chain should be ethical and workers should be treated fairly. It is important to consider all stakeholders and everyone involved, including the staff, the consumers and the supply chain.

How important is it for businesses to give back to the community?

I think it is incredibly important for a business to give back to the community for several reasons. First of all, if you take from a community, you should give back. I believe the businesses that stand the test of time are reciprocal to all stakeholders and work with those with a vested interest in the business. Second, I believe as humans, it is our responsibility to try and create equality – that is the only way to create collective change. If only a few participate, it will take longer. Third, the later generations, especially Gen Z, have a vested interest in businesses that have a social and moral compass. A corporate social responsibility department is no longer good enough; it has to run through the veins of a company. Furthermore, transparency is inevitable, whether you like it or not, in this age due to the internet and social media; if your business does not stand with and work with integrity, it will come out one day.

Finally, and not the reason you should do it, I have found that in giving back, many more are willing to give to me – opportunities, a helping hand and more. Those who give with their heart often receive in abundance, even in business.

How do you measure the success of your business mission?

There are various different ways to measure the success of a business mission. My favourite is the use of case studies to evidence the qualitative value of the work we do and tracking what our young people go on to achieve. There are also other tools such as social auditing, the outcome matrix, the theory of change and more – something we need to update at the moment!

---

6. Be a problem-solving leader

Of course, it's one thing to have identified a problem and found a solution with your business; it's another to become the kind of leader that is able to effectively carry out that solution. So much of business is about the leadership and direction that the founder drives through the company, so let's look at a few ways that you can step into being a problem-solving leader:

↳ Use your own **emotional intelligence.** To understand the needs and wants of our audience, we must use our own emotional intelligence to empathize with others. The more personal you can make your business, the better. Recognize in yourself the frustrations or emotions you feel when faced with this particular problem. Try to avoid making assumptions about your audience – recognize your own emotional patterns, use those emotions to guide you and see if you can spot those patterns in others.

↳ Practise **curiosity.** I think staying curious is so important for business – it's often our curiosity that leads us into a new project or venture and can open up new doors. Sometimes curiosity is the only feeling you've got, before passion, drive or commitment to an idea, so don't overlook staying curious – it's often the place that the best ideas come from. Take a little longer pondering how to solve a problem than you would normally, practise research and define the problem, being led by your own personal curiosity.

↳ Get familiar with **asking questions**. It's amazing how much you can learn about your target customer by simply getting in the habit of asking questions – whether that's on social media or face-to-face, given the opportunity, it's so important to get in the head of your consumer. Things like focus groups, tasting and demonstrations, webinars or surveys are just a few of the ways you can be regularly asking questions of your audience. I find nothing really beats the power of in-person dialogue with your audience, so creating opportunities to talk in person is so powerful for driving your business.

↳ Learn to listen through **creative brainstorming**. When brain-storming with a team, try to create an environment where everyone listens and is heard – a space where no idea is too silly, and everyone feels they can contribute. Creating a 'safe space' for brainstorming is so important because it's often where the best ideas happen.

↳ Be **positive** in the face of a challenge and create **smaller goals**. Sometimes a problem can seem huge and overwhelming – for example if you're trying to create a business that tackles climate change – so try to focus in on one aspect of the larger problem that you think you can affect, such as making one product more sustainable. Start small and find a niche within a larger problem to make the process less overwhelming.

7. Communicate your message

Once you have identified your message, it's time to communicate it effectively to your consumer. I think communication is particularly relevant for solution-focused businesses, as you're often trying to get your customers to change their habits – whether that's behavioural, spending or shopping habits. Communication of your message, and why people should spend with you, is so important!

TOP TIPS: COMMUNICATING YOUR MESSAGE

I asked Eloise Leeson, a trained linguist and communications specialist, to share her advice. Eloise cut her teeth working with brands like Deliveroo, Edinburgh Gin, and BrewDog. She's now the founder of Olim Comms, where she works to help businesses close the gap between what they think they're saying, and what's *actually* being received by their customers. Here's her top tips for communicating with your consumers:

1. Figure out what the heck you're actually trying to say!

This is a big one. So many people are focused either on talking for the sake of it, or because they think they have to talk lots to be relevant. Don't let the truth of your message get muddied by quantity, and instead, focus on the quality of your output.

It's tempting to dilute yourself down to be 'palatable', or to dial yourself up to 11 and be extreme, but the message that's best for *your* audience is the one that is true to you. Don't waste time with anything else.

2. Do your research

You figured out what you want to say – awesome! Now comes the time to do your research into how that message is best received.

Do some digging into your audience, their likes and dislikes, and the way they want to receive your message. Does your audience prefer written text to videos, or infographics over Instagram stories?

Now you test! Yes, it's terrifying, but you need to try lots of different things to see what works. Fail fast, and figure it out quickly, so you can keep moving forward in the right direction. You've got a finite amount of time and energy, so it pays to narrow your focus on what's *really* working for people. You can test

---

whether your messaging is working through regularly surveying your audience (such as through Instagram stories), asking for feedback and checking your analytics. Ultimately, you want your messaging to be converting into sales, so that's the real test!

3. There's no silver bullet for a solid-gold reputation

Consumers' trust is harder to come by than ever before in a market flooded with competition and cynicism. Transparency and honesty are crucial when communicating with an audience (and having that audience is a privilege, not a given), so use these as watchwords when you're creating content of any kind.

A solid-gold reputation is an antidote to cynicism, and that's won by genuinely engaging with your audience and taking real interest in them as individuals. How do you do that? Listen, listen, listen – *then* respond.

4. Engage from a place of authenticity, *not* perfection

Authenticity gets lobbed about a lot – but what does it actually mean? To be authentic is to be true to **all** of yourself. It's about being genuine, and that inspires loyalty.

So when you're communicating, ditch the idea of being perfect, and embrace your uniqueness instead. That might mean the odd typo on Facebook, or a stutter during a presentation – but it shows that you're real and human, and that fosters the best kind of connection.

5. Remember it's a human-to-human interaction – *always*

Speaking of being human – the very best way to communicate effectively with your audience is to treat every chance you get to speak with them as a real human-to-human interaction – even if it's on the other side of a screen.

There's a temptation to treat people as a means to an end, to hustle, to write hard-core sales copy, and focus on the transaction – but honestly, as a customer yourself, could you think of anything more alienating?

Focus instead on forging real human connection by treating everyone with dignity and respect – and trust that the right transactions will take care of themselves.

I hope in this chapter you've gained some insight into how you can make your brand and business more problem-facing and translating that message far and wide. There's a few more questions to consider in the workbook below to go even deeper into your company's approach.

WORKBOOK

Q1: Do I now have a clearer sense of what problem I'm trying to solve with my business?

_____

_____

_____

Q2: What are the biggest challenges with trying to solve this problem? That is, am I looking to change people's behaviour and habits?

_____

_____

_____

_____

Q3: How do I feel about facing new, unexpected challenges in my business? How can I give myself the best chance of overcoming problems and becoming solution-focused?

_____

_____

_____

_____

Q4: How am I going to communicate my message to my audience? What strategy will I put in place to talk authentically to my audience?

_____

_____

_____

_____

CASE STUDY   She Made It: Saasha Celestial-One

Name: Saasha Celestial-One
Job title: Co-founder and COO of OLIO

How did the idea for your business come about?

The inspiration for OLIO came when my good friend and co-founder, Tessa Cook, was moving back from abroad and found herself with some perfectly good sweet potatoes and cabbage, which the removal men would not let her pack. After unsuccessfully looking for someone on the street to share her bounty with, she ended up smuggling the produce in her bags rather than letting them go to waste. Once back in the UK, she lamented that there must be an easier way to share food, and I thought she was on to an amazing idea that I wanted to help bring to life. Within an hour we had chosen a name and OLIO was born.

What problem are you trying to solve with your business?

We're solving the scandal of food waste, which plays an enormous role in the climate crisis – a consortia of the world's leading climate change scientists recently ranked the top 100 solutions to the climate crisis, and reducing food waste came in at number 1, above solar power and electric cars. OLIO solves the problem of food waste in the home by making it easy and fun for everyday people to share their spare food with people living nearby.

How did you raise finance for it? How was the process of raising investment as a woman?

Tessa and I bootstrapped for the first nine months but have since raised four rounds from venture capitalists and impact funds. Female-founded teams receive only 1 per cent of available investment, so it did feel like the odds were stacked against us. However, we found we had much greater cut-through when pitching to female investors (the majority of our users are female too, so this makes sense).

A lot of founders underestimate how much work fundraising is. In reality, it's a full-time job, so we're constantly liaising with new and existing investors and planning for the next raise, even if it's 18 months away. For example, we proactively define in advance which milestones we need to hit to raise successfully, so we stay laser-focused on that from an execution perspective.

What are some of the biggest challenges facing sustainability-focused businesses?

The main challenge is getting people to change their behaviour away from the status quo in order to have the impact we're after. At OLIO we not only need to persuade people that our current food system (massive waste and food poverty) is no longer acceptable, but we also need to convince them to change their food-sharing and consumption routines. This is why finding the *right* investors has been so important for us – investors who understand that patient capital is required to bring about mainstream behaviour change.

Any advice on what is and isn't worth spending money on at the start?

At OLIO we hate waste of all kinds, so we've always been resourceful with our budget. Also, our team has been 'remote first' from the beginning, so we haven't spent unnecessarily on office overhead. Being remote has meant we can recruit for exceptional talent from all over the world and hire employees who would have been out of geographic reach if we had a traditional office.

What was your first hire and why?

Our first hire was a woman named Viv, who joined as our 'one stop shop' for all things marketing, analytics and growth. Five years later, Viv is still with us, and currently heads the product team, an area she's grown into. We hired Viv because she had a rare blend of creative and analytical strengths, and we were looking for someone with the energy and flexibility to scale with us as we grew. Above all, we hired her (and the 30 employees that have followed since) because she is as mission-obsessed as Tessa and I. You can train people for skills, but you can't train passion.

How did you overcome the challenges the global pandemic threw your way?

COVID-19 has been a bit of a rollercoaster, both personally and professionally. At the beginning of lockdown, it wasn't at all clear that a neighbour-to-neighbour food-sharing app could continue to operate! However, after speaking with our food safety lawyer, environmental health officer, and community, it quickly became apparent that we had a responsibility to ensure that OLIO *could* continue to operate as so many people were depending upon us as a lifeline.

We then had a frantic few weeks communicating to our users how the app would work (introducing 'no-contact pickups' was key) and supporting our business partners whose stores were closing. As a result, the amount of food saved from businesses doubled in the first 30 days of COVID-19 versus the previous 30 days.

What can we do to encourage more women entrepreneurs?

Attending events and being open to sharing your learnings and making introductions to personal networks is a good place to start. Also, I spend an hour or so a week taking calls from other female founders who are keen to learn from our journey, and I like to think that's very helpful to them.

CHAPTER TWELVE

Making your business stand out from the crowd

In this chapter, we're going to be looking at your business offering and how you can make it stand out in a crowded marketplace. We'll also be discovering how to find the unique voice of your brand to make it shine.

Uniqueness doesn't always come from having a never-been-seen-before product or service, but from the way in which you *package* it – how you make it stand out from others, using your brand expression, presence and personality.

In my experience, many of the successful female entrepreneurs I know have not necessarily re-invented the wheel, but they have brought a *fresh* take to something established. You don't always have to conceive something new, but you might be able to bring an exciting slant on an existing product or service.

Essentially, being an entrepreneur is about being able to envision something amazing and improve on the work of those who have gone before, which relies on excellent messaging, communication and branding.

Before we dive into messaging, let's figure out the ways in which your business is different from those currently in the marketplace.

EXERCISE: DISCOVERING YOUR UNIQUE SELLING POINT

Grab a pen and paper, and spend some time thinking about the questions below:

What makes your business different from others in the marketplace currently?

What have you seen in the current marketplace that you don't like?

What do you think you can do better than those in the same space?

What legacy would you like to leave behind with your business?

How do you want your customer to feel having used your product or service?

What inspires you to create this business? What difference are you trying to make to the lives of your consumers?

Are there any businesses, in your industry or another, that you think are doing things really well and why?

Standing out from the crowd

There are a few things that I've learned about standing out from the crowd when it comes to launching your own business. The main one is this: don't give yourself a hard time if you don't feel like your offering is currently unique enough. Not every business is going to solve a problem or invent something new. What you can do, however, is deliver absolutely excellent customer service, nail your brand's voice or build a community around your business that keeps it exciting.

There are loads of things you can do to create points of differentiation between your brand and others, even though the offering might be similar to another. Here are a few top tips from me about distinguishing your business from others':

Deliver exemplary customer service

We now live in a world where brilliant customer service is expected, as we have more access than ever before to touch-points with brands – including being able to call them out when the customer service does not live up to standards! Thanks to social media, if we're disappointed with a company, we can use our voice publicly to draw attention to them, so we have to be extra careful to deliver great customer service.

Social media can have such a positive impact for brands; I've seen so many amazing female-owned businesses that use social media to connect deeply with their audience and get feedback on their offering – it's one great way that new challenger brands can 'break through' and do something fresh compared with estab-lished brands.

Of course, this is not the only reason why customer service should be at the heart of your business – you want to create genuine and real connections with your audience, so you can get repeat customers and build trust and loyalty with your consumer. Great customer service is as much for you as it is for your customer.

Solve your customer pain points

To create a business that feels unique, you need to get in the head of your customer to understand their pain points and any frus-trations they feel using other companies of a similar kind.

For example, you might find that you can create a unique offering in the way that you deliver a product or be able to offer more flexibility with your offering than others in the market-place. By asking a customer about their pain points in the market research stage of your business, you'll be able to create some-thing that understands them truly. Here are some questions that can be useful to ask when discovering your customers' pain points:

↪ What do you currently find frustrating about this product/service?
↪ What feels antiquated to you?
↪ What puts you off purchasing this product/service?
↪ What would you like to see a challenger brand do in the marketplace?

Dare to be different

If you've seen something that another company has done, which you haven't liked, that's the impetus to do things better. Similarly, you can be inspired by the boldness of other brands. Being bold is important – often doing things differently is having the *confidence* to do them differently. Be bold in your ambitions. Believe in yourself to create change.

Focus on a niche

Get really clear on the audience you're trying to attract and create that niche for yourself. You need to get specific about the age, demographic, location and income of your ideal customer, and try to find a new niche if you're launching a business in a very competitive space.

For example, your business may not be something totally new, but you might be trying to bring this business to a younger audience. Focusing on a niche is a great way to give your business clarity and have something to measure against, to see if you're attracting the target customer for your company.

Create a great offer

One way to make your company stand out in a crowded marketplace is by offering enticing offers and policies for your customers that reflect the values of your brand. For example, perhaps you can offer year-long returns on products or a 30-day money-back guarantee. With a service-based business, you might like to create a bespoke welcome pack for your clients that has a personal touch. A 'strong' offering is one that feels unique and exceptional to your company alone – here are a few more ideas of interesting offerings you can make:

Product-based businesses

We all know that introductory discounts work well for companies, such as 10 per cent off your first order, but I think to really stand out there's new things you can do to draw in customers:

↪ Enticing referral schemes when you invite others to use the company. For example, Classpass gives you £40 off when a friend joins (and they get a special discount!), meaning you both benefit.

↪ Special discounts on your birthday, which makes the company feels more personalized.

↪ A free gift with your first order – something small but perhaps a keepsake that will remind you of the brand.

↪ A regular discount that you roll out weekly/monthly, such as a Friday Favourites deal – this helps customers get into the flow of your business and expect correspondence from you.

Service-based businesses

When it comes to service-based business, the best way to stand out is to make your offering better – more personal, efficient, results-oriented – than others in the market. This comes down to really focusing in on the benefits the clients will receive by working with you. Here are a few things you can do as a service business to create a great offering:

↪ Create a unique launch offer when you introduce any new programmes or offerings. For example, going beyond the standard introductory discount, could you offer an extra special discount for the first 10 people who sign up to your course? Think of fresh ways to incentivize sales and orders.

↪ Brainstorm low-risk ways that clients can try out your service, such as a complimentary introductory call, a discounted first session or free appraisal. Of course, you have to be wary of undervaluing your services and giving away too much for free, but finding ways to draw people in is important if you're trying to get new clients.

↪ Think of ways you can create a long-term relationship with your customer. Could you create a unique course or offering only for clients who have previously worked with you? Could you offer a special rate for those you've worked with before? Find ways to reward repeat clients and encourage them to work with you again.

↪ Create a bespoke welcome pack for your clients. As mentioned previously, anything personalized or hand-written is a great way to add a personal touch. If you can create something that's standardized across the board for anyone that works with you, it will help create your own brand style.

Create a vibrant company culture

Of course, another way of thinking about how you can make your company stand out in a crowded marketplace is how you can create change internally that will be reflected in the output and ethos of your brand. Creating a great company culture – a place where people want to work and are passionate about the product they are building – will show up in so many positive ways for your business. By creating a culture where everyone feels seen and heard, with great policies like flexible and remote working, your team will be incentivized to work hard and be challenged. If you'd like your business to stand out in a crowded marketplace for your customer, think about how your company can stand out from others internally too – shifting the dial internally will help bring fresh energy and creativity to your business.

Think about cause marketing

Cause marketing is where you give back to a non-profit or cause through your company – it's a great way to bring more purpose and good to your business and align yourself with a cause that reflects your internal values. If there's a cause you're particularly passionate about, why not include it in your business model to add depth and good to your business? Of course, this needs to be something that feels true and honest to you – but it can be a great way to stand out in a crowded marketplace and show a compassionate side to your business.

Become a social business

You could even take this one step further and become a social business. As consumers become increasingly savvy about the devastating effects that consumerism and big businesses can have on the world – from environmental damage and landfill to fair pay and modern-day slavery – we're looking to buy more and more from brands that show they *care*.

Whether it's donating a portion of your profits to a worthy cause or even setting up your business as a non-profit, think about what values you truly want your work to honour and how that can be reflected in the structure of your company.

Don't be afraid of being different

Quirky is wonderful, especially in business. I think often we're afraid of being quirky, of standing out. But in business, you need to be a little different. When you think outside of the box with your marketing strategy and allow yourself to get a little uncomfortable, great things can happen. When I say quirky, what I mean is adopting an unconventional way of thinking about your business and its offering. This is why different is good:

↳ Quirky is rare. When your company does things differently, you've already got a competitive advantage because your offering is more valuable because it's rarer to find.

↳ Quirky is harder to copy. If you make your brand stand out, it's harder to imitate, because there's no one quite like you. The value of your product or business automatically starts to decrease the second your consumer realizes there's an alternative out there at a lower cost, so being 'weird' stops you being copied so easily.

↳ Quirky gets you noticed. Fitting in, often, makes you invisible. You look like all your competitors. There's nothing to set you apart. Being weird, however, makes you super visible because there's no one quite like you. Of course, you want to make sure you're attracting the right kind of attention – but being noticed is always better than blending in.

↳ Quirky is surprising. Surprise and delight is an important part of business – going above and beyond for your customers to give them an extra special experience with your company. By being weird, you have more room to surprise your audience and create an emotional response with them, which will keep them feeling connected and, hopefully, passionate about your brand.

Add personalized elements to your business

I absolutely love a business that's able to offer a personalized element to their offering. I think we should be continually looking for ways to surprise, delight AND reward customers for their loyalty – and thinking differently about ways to incorporate personalized elements to your business is a must for standing out. Here are a few ideas of personalized elements you may like to include with your business:

FOR PRODUCT BUSINESSES

↳ a hand-written note in your order;
↳ offering customization to the product, such as embossing or personalizing;
↳ creating bespoke offers for return customers;

↳ offering made-to-order products;

↳ implement a loyalty programme.

FOR SERVICE BUSINESSES

↳ offer multiple customer service channels, such as WhatsApp;

↳ hand-written correspondence, such as thank you cards;

↳ sending a gift to mark a special occasion;

↳ using first names for correspondence – it's a small thing but makes a big difference;

↳ personalized email marketing, ie segment lists for different kinds of clients.

Hopefully this chapter has given you some inspiration on how you can make your business stand out in a crowded marketplace. Below are a few workbook questions to answer, which will help you dive even deeper into the unique offering of your brand.

WORKBOOK

Q1: What have you learned about standing out from the crowd in this chapter?

_____

_____

_____

_____

Q2: What are the things you think make your business unique that you've now learned?

_____

_____

_____

_____

Q3: What are you going to do to make your business stand out?

_____

_____

_____

_____

Q4: What personalized elements can you bring to your business to draw in new customers and clients?

_____

_____

_____

_____

Q5: What makes you nervous about trying to stand out from the crowd and how can you overcome these mental blocks? What would be the benefits of standing out?

_____

_____

_____

_____

_____

Your toolkit for success

In Part Three of *She Made It*, I'm going to equip you with the digital tools you need to market your business and reach a bigger audience. The internet has provided so many opportunities for founders to grow their business (largely for free!), but with an ever-changing landscape, you need to stay on top of the latest trends and tricks in digital marketing.

In this final section of the book, we're going to be looking at how to build your personal brand and use social media, content, PR and community-focused events to amplify your business offering. We'll be looking at the latest trends in social media and speaking to influencers and industry experts who use social media to boost their profile, income and brand value, whilst staying authentic. PR is another huge topic that we'll be deep-diving into, looking at ways that you can make your business more press-worthy and gain attention from the media. Kicking off this section, let's look at personal brand and how it can strengthen your business reach.

CHAPTER THIRTEEN

Creating a personal brand

What do we mean when we talk about *personal brand*, and do you need one? Personal brand is the practice of marketing yourself. Essentially, it's self-packaging how you communicate yourself to the world. Personal brand is the 21st-century version of traditional advertising – where you focus on the brand of *you*.

There is no doubt that consumers are becoming increasingly interested in *personal* narratives, rather than corporate ones – we're obsessed with following each other's lives, successes and careers online. We want to know what drives you, inspires you and why you do the work that you do. Why are Instagram stories so popular? Because people want to see behind the scenes of your daily work; when the curtain falls, what's left behind?

This is particularly relevant if you are the face of the company or a freelancer trying to attract more clients. Making your brand as personal as possible keeps it accessible and inclusive – and gives you creative ways to highlight your *why*.

What's more, understanding your personal brand helps structure your content strategy and align your business. Figure out your values and personal passions and you'll be able to carve a narrative around yourself – these feed into your content output.

Personal brand: the benefits

Still unsure? Let's look at the main reasons why cultivating a personal brand is important today:

→ **Personal brand gives you autonomy.** One thing I really like about creating a strong personal brand is that it's something no one can take away. When you work for a company, your identity is often linked to that particular job role and title. Hence, you're relevant to people for as long as you're in that job. But who stays in a job forever? If you focus on building a personal brand, one that's uniquely your own, it gives you a power over your career.

→ **Personal brand is the modern-day CV.** Having a personal brand is like an amazing CV that you can broadcast to your audience for free. Personal brand drives your content narrative; the more content you put online, the more positive messaging there is online about you.

→ **Personal brand brings you more work.** You get a sense of ownership with building up your own personal brand – which makes you attractive to potential clients or future employers, as it sets you apart. Here are a few things that have permanence online: social media, Google news, blog posts about you, podcasts and press. If you can achieve these things with your name in, you're already on your way to internet success.

→ **Personal brand helps a portfolio career.** Having a personal brand allows you to do more things at once. We're in an age now of portfolio careers – with several part-time jobs or a series of jobs, rather than full-time employment – and personal brand feeds well into that. By being known for your values, not just the work you do, brands and potential clients will think of you more laterally – you'll be considered for work you never dreamed of because of the values and expertise you hold. This could include speaking opportunities, brand consultancy, featuring on podcasts or media appearances. When you have a strong personal brand, people get you. They like you. They align with your values. Through connecting with the deeper purpose of your brand, you'll become industry-agnostic and your portfolio career will flourish.

↪ **Personal brand builds trust with your audience.** Business is a people-centric game; those we choose to work with, to trust, to hire – it's all about people. Thanks to social media, we've moved into a more people-centric world than ever before. Now employers and customers can look at personal snaps of you on Facebook, your endorsements on LinkedIn and your workouts on Instagram Stories. This move towards people-centric business is as much an opportunity as it is a disadvantage – it's the chance to put people at the heart of your business, and leverage trust in a world of online accounts. Putting authenticity and honesty at the core of your work will help you grow and flourish online.

Expert guide: understanding your personal brand

How do you actually build a personal brand? I've developed a simple formula for building a personal brand, which has helped generate us over 100,000 followers on social media, featured in national newspapers and host sell-out festivals. Let's dive in.

Overview: creating your personal brand

Understanding how you can stand out is beneficial for three reasons. First, if you've built your personal brand in a way that makes you stand out from others, it means that you're simply the right choice for certain projects, because you're the *only* choice. You're uniquely you. You offer something totally different from others in your industry. Your experience separates you from others. Find something that sets you apart from others, and you're safeguarding your future.

Another reason that standing out is important is that it shields you against price discounting. If you're a brand unto yourself, you set the price in a way that reflects your skill, value and experience. Your pricing is linked to your self-esteem – it's the value you put on what you think you're worth to the world. If you can create a personal brand that sets you apart from others in your industry, you're in a strong position *not* to discount your price – even when others are. You can charge what you like, because there is no one quite like you.

Finally, if you can find the thing that sets you apart, it's a great barrier against clients going to competitors. You become sought-after in your industry. By being memorable, hopefully for the proven record of your work, you diminish the power of the competition – by simply being you, and doing you well, you will put yourself in a different league. I encourage you not to let the thought of competitors stop you from taking a leap into the unknown; your competitors are not spending their days worrying about you, and you shouldn't let the fear of their presence stop you from pursuing your dreams. If you're confident enough in what you uniquely offer, don't let competition hold you back.

What you're looking for, in essence, is sustained fame in your local market – this might be geographically, or in your professional category. By fame, I mean fans – fans, followers, likes, clients, anyone who actively engages with your work and follows what you're doing. The more fans you have, the stronger your personal brand is. There are four things you need to build your brand, which I've summarized below.

Building blocks of your personal brand

There are four main building blocks of a personal brand in my opinion:

1. Focus on your personal story

It doesn't help you to be a generalist when it comes to personal brand. Focus on what makes you... you. What's unique about your story that feeds into your work? What's unique about your experience? What are you passionate about? Focus in on something that makes you interesting; this might be your heritage, your belief system, your skill.

Why is it important to have a focus? Because it's easier for you to draw individuals into your business or work if you know what your focus is. Also, the marketplace will be able to identify you more easily if you've got a clear focus. Here are a few pointers on how you can focus on the personal elements of your story:

↪ **Passion** – is there something you're passionate about that could translate well into an online brand? For example, maybe you're a chef whose passion is for creating amazing plant-based recipes. This will help your social media feeds stand out from others and help grow your following by tapping into the vegan community online.

↪ **Heritage** – is there a part of your heritage that influences your work today? Don't shy away from that heritage; use it to give vibrancy to your career. You may connect with something that's authentic to your personal heritage and will also create a niche to help you stand out.

↪ **Experience** – did something happen to you that changed the course of your life? Did an experience lead to a career change? Perhaps there's an interesting backstory that led you to creating this business or career. Use your personal experiences to build a narrative around yourself.

↪ **Skill** – do you have a skill that others don't, which could help you stand out? For example, you're a fantastic live illustrator, gluten-free baker or website coder. Understand what makes you different from others in your industry; this unique viewpoint will make your content interesting and appealing.

2. Show your enthusiasm

Are you enthusiastic about the work you're doing? The best way to create enthusiasm with your audience is by showing your own. Don't undervalue your work with language that doesn't reflect your passion – talk in terms of your passions – use language to describe your work that conveys what you're passionate about, what fires you up and gets you out of bed in the morning.

3. Don't forget to network!

I know networking can sometimes seem a little overwhelming, so a good place to start is networking in your own community; that could be in your industry, the area you live in or engaging with the followers you already have online.

Networking is an important part of business, because you never know the outcome; it allows you to meet new people, hopefully create connections, and takes you in new directions. You have to put yourself in interesting situations for interesting things to happen to you.

4. Build up a circle of influence

One of the key aspects of having a personal brand is the assumption that you influence decisions and trends in your industry. We all have circles of influence, and the idea is to build these up more and more, as our personal brand grows. The easiest place to start is to build a circle of influence in your immediate community – this might be your local area, or others in your industry who you already know. You don't need to be an 'influencer' with thousands of followers online to influence people; you might have only 200 followers, but they could be 200 of the most engaged, important accountants in your industry, for example. It's not always a numbers game.

Ask yourself how you can boost your personal circles of influence – this might be partnering with someone else in your industry for cross-promotional social media or blog content. Name association can really help boost your influence, so suggest becoming an 'expert' in your guide for someone else's blog or publication. Everyone wants to boost their work – if you come with knowledge and skill, you can provide something to further their brand whilst promoting your own. Influence is one of the core pillars of personal brand; consider who you want to influence, and the best way to go about building this influence in an organic and natural way for your brand.

WORKBOOK

Q1: How can I stand out and be memorable? How can I cut through the noise of my industry?

_____
_____
_____
_____

Q2: Where should I focus my attention? What's special about me? Why am I different?

_____
_____
_____
_____

Q3: What am I enthusiastic about? What are my main interests and how do these feed into the work I'm doing?

_____

_____

_____

_____

Q4: What are my main networking opportunities? What do I want to achieve from networking?

_____

_____

_____

_____

Q5: What are my main circles of influence? Who do I want to influence and why?

_____

_____

_____

_____

How to build a personal brand

Now you understand the core elements of a personal brand – focus, enthusiasm, networking and influence – let's look at how best to communicate these to your audience.

The way I see it, personal brand begins within – it's the stuff that fires you up, excites and motivates you – and the output is how you show your audience that fire. Here are my top tips for how to communicate your personal brand values:

Blogging

Blogging generates search engine optimization (SEO) on your name and furthers your personal brand by ranking for certain keywords online. Having control over the positive content that goes out on the internet with your name on is invaluable; it's an opportunity to set yourself up as an authority in your field. Basically, blogging is like a portfolio you can create for yourself at no cost.

Where should you write? In my view, the best place to write online is a website in your own name. It's so valuable to have your own website – this is your own little real estate on the internet, where you can carve your niche. If you don't think you have time to maintain a personal website, look at writing for Huffington Post, or a popular website within your industry. Here are a few pointers for blogging for personal brand:

↪ **Opinion** – do you have a strong opinion on a topic that you can convey eloquently and convincingly? This is a mission statement in personal brand – letting your readers know what you're all about.

↪ **Facts** – do you hold facts on something in the zeitgeist or news cycle? Using research or facts really helps amplify blog content and offers something different on popular topics across the internet.

↪ **Multimedia content** – what else can you offer, beyond words, to make your blog content interesting? If you've got additional skills at your disposal – video, illustrator, Photoshop, podcasting – *use* them. The more multimedia content on your site, the better.

Social media

It's great if all your content can flow with each other; your blog feeds into your social, which feeds into your imagery and email marketing. You want everything to be a fluid, harmonious relationship. Social content is key to your personal brand – and frankly, this alone is enough to build your circles of influence. You can 'blog' on Instagram, LinkedIn, Facebook, etc, through captions alone – in the next chapter, I'll be sharing my insights on how to use social media effectively for your career.

Email marketing

Why not create a newsletter with your latest career happenings? Here are a few ideas for what can go on your personal brand newsletter:

↳ links to recent articles you've written;

↳ links to any media coverage you've had;

↳ links to podcasts you've recorded;

↳ articles you've found interesting;

↳ events you're talking at;

↳ your social media handles.

Use MailChimp to design something that's aesthetically pleasing and engaging – their analytics can really help you understand what's working best for your audience and create a newsletter that helps reach the most people.

Video and imagery

Video is a great way to supercharge your personal brand. High-quality video highlighting your work and who you are, on the homepage of your personal website, is a great way to give people a real insight into your personal brand. I wouldn't shy away from the things that normally make you cringe; video marketing is a fantastic introduction to your authentic self.

Proper headshots are so important. Make sure you've got great-quality imagery of yourself on your website, which is super professional and reflective of you. When it comes to blogging, make sure you've got good-quality imagery to support your writing – it's often what draws the reader in.

WORKBOOK

Q1: Does blogging work for me? What can I blog about?

_____

_____

_____

Q2: What do I want to promote on my social feeds?

_____

_____

_____

_____

Q3: Can I create an email newsletter to send out? What can I feature on it?

_____

_____

_____

_____

Q4: Could I produce a video for my website? What would I say on the video?

_____

_____

_____

_____

Q5: Do I have good-quality imagery for my website and social feeds?

_____

_____

_____

Four ways to supercharge your personal brand

Now here are a few hacks for supercharging your personal brand that I've found have really helped me with About Time. These will give your brand a big boost:

Produce an event

There is no quicker way to get your name and face in front of the masses than producing an event. It doesn't need be a huge-scale event – something that feels manageable and realistic to you but which can draw in a crowd. We've hosted over 100 events at About Time, and it's been a fantastic way to meet our audience and build brand credibility. Consider the following ideas:

> ↳ **Host a panel talk** – this is a great way to align yourself with other 'influencers' and experts in your industry, making yourself part of a movement. We've found a maximum of four speakers on a panel works best, and if you host it yourself, you have the advantage of becoming a linchpin between great minds in your industry.

> ↳ **Host an experience** – this could be a yoga class, a glass-blowing workshop, a masterclass in self-assessment tax returns. Basically, if you have knowledge and skill to share, why not create an event out of it? This helps your audience interact with you in a more meaningful way and will attract future brands to work with you.

> ↳ **Host a networking event** – this one's easy to do and has great results. Why not host an informal networking event for your industry? This could be something as simple as a dinner party, breakfast or after-work drinks in a local pub. It's a great way to build personal circles of influence and bring people together in your name.

Get in the press

Media exposure is a great way to boost your personal brand. Positioning yourself as an 'expert' on a topic will help garner media attention – the best way to earn this expertise is through the above output, including blog, social, events and email marketing. Regular features on topics in the news cycle are the best way to get yourself noticed by the press, who are regularly looking for experts to comment on a news story or trend. Increase your visibility to the press, and the opportunities will start rolling in naturally.

Start a podcast

A podcast is a simply fantastic way to super-charge your personal brand. If you buy your own podcast equipment and learn how to do a simple edit, it's almost a cost-free way to boost your public profile. You can invite interesting guests on to your show and align yourself with other influencers in your industry to boost your name. Come up with an interesting, original premise for the show and spread it far and wide.

Publish a book

You know what, you don't even need a publisher. What about writing your own e-book on a topic that you know well or partnering with other 'experts' to create a manual for your industry. The word 'author' carries such power and kudos, this will really help boost your profile. Think of a topic that hasn't been extensively covered in your industry and find a niche to exploit.

WORKBOOK

Q1: Can I host an event? What kind of event excites me to produce?

_____

_____

_____

Q2: How can I increase my visibility for the media? What kind of media do I see myself being featured on?

_____

_____

_____

_____

Q3: What kind of podcast would I like to produce? Would this help me? What do I need to get the podcast going?

_____

_____

_____

_____

Q4: Can I write a book? What would it be about and where do I see it being published?

_____

_____

_____

_____

CASE STUDY   She Made It: Alice Benham

Name: Alice Benham

Job title: Digital marketing coach and entrepreneur

How did you get into the work you're doing now?

I left school at 17 for my first freelance role in social media management. With my naive enthusiasm in hand, I said yes to every opportunity that came my way but was burnt out after nine months. After that, I realized I wanted to expand into digital marketing as a whole but teach others how to do it, not do it for them. Cue the start of the business I have now – digital marketing support for female entrepreneurs.

How did you have the confidence to launch your business and new offerings?

Honest answer – I just went for it! I knew that for people to invest in me I'd need to believe in myself, so I put my head down, learned everything through experience and let my confidence grow as the business did.

How important is social media to your work?

It's everything! It's the main way my business grows and the primary thing I help people with. The business I have now wouldn't exist without it! The opportunity it presents to grow an audience with value and connection at the forefront is remarkable.

What advice would you give people wanting to grow their audience and engagement on social media?

Focus on the value you can bring. If you share value (information, entertainment, relatability, inspiration, etc) that is relevant to your ideal client or customer, the audience growth and end sales will flow. Nobody would read a newspaper if it was purely advertising. The same can be said for our social media accounts!

Five top tips for Instagram growth

- Serve before you sell.
- Create a clear purpose to your account and utilize your bio to communicate that.
- Harness the growth that comes with creating 'shareable' content.
- Allow your personality to shine through.
- Respond to your audience when they comment and message.

When it comes to creating content for your business, what should you be considering? Which platforms and why?

You don't have to be on every platform; focus on the ones where (1) your ideal customer/client is, and (2) your message is well suited to the format.

How careful should you be about being too 'salesy' when creating content?

In a country where we're sensitive about being sold to, very! It's a fine balance between creating intentionally and sounding salesy. My content is constantly selling to people, but it rarely feels that way. I do that by building my online presence through value-led story-telling that is constantly reminding people what I do, the value I bring and how they can engage in that.

Are podcasts still a good way to amplify your brand?

Absolutely! The popularity of podcasts are continually growing and the ability to get people tuning into long-form content (ie more than just a tweet or Instagram story) is invaluable.

Do you think 'personal brand' is still relevant?

Absolutely – the phrase 'people buy from people' is true now more than ever. When content is created through the lens of a person, it's far more engaging and relatable to the audience. A personal brand isn't about selling your soul for content but utilizing your humanity to build connection with an audience.

How important is tone of voice and how do you go about creating your unique voice?

You find your voice by using it, not thinking about it. Your tone of voice is a constantly evolving thing and, like any muscle, the more you use it, the stronger it gets. Like your visual identity (branding), tone of voice is what brings continuity between your platforms and familiarity to your audience.

What do you think holds women back the most when it comes to launching their own businesses?

Starting. Big dreams are great, but when those dreams feel wildly different from where you are now, it can be hard to take action. There's no magic formula or five-step plan to starting a business – it's the non-linear combination of daily uncomfortable action. It doesn't really matter how or where you start – what matters is that you do.

CHAPTER FOURTEEN

Social media to supercharge your business

I have learned so much about the power of social media in my six years of running About Time and I'm so excited to share my insights in this chapter with you. Social media has been crucial to our business; it's how we've built up our audience, grown website traffic, developed brand loyalty, promoted our events and attracted brand partnerships.

It's at the heart of everything we do and investing time in social media shouldn't be an after-thought for any business. But social media can be overwhelming for new businesses – questions such as which platforms to be on, how often to post, how to increase your followers and *what* to post are things I'm asked time and time again at our events.

We've organically built our audience on social media to over 100,000 users across platforms, and in this chapter, I'm going to show you how you can grow your audience, engagement and following too.

BUSINESS VERSUS PERSONAL ACCOUNTS

Something I'm asked about a lot is whether you should have a personal account, as well as one for your business. For me, the answer is always YES! A personal account allows you to show the behind-the-scenes of your work, which people love, and makes your brand and journey more accessible.

As a founder, I'd always recommend having a separate account for you personally – this will help build your personal brand. I've found that building engagement on my personal Twitter and Instagram accounts is actually easier than the brand one, as our audience love seeing the journey of our business. Don't be afraid of putting yourself front and centre of your business – often the most interesting thing about your business is YOU! The tips below are useful for both brand and personal accounts, as I believe the same rules apply across for all social media.

Social media: the core principles

Before adopting any growth strategy, however, it's important to ask yourself what you're trying to achieve through social media. Let's first look at the core principles of social media that should support any content strategy – here are my pillars of savvy social media:

Truth

The word 'authenticity' is overused, and I think we can go a step further and say that social media is about showing your *truth*. There will be things that are true and real to you – it might be your passion for your business, travel or motherhood – which you can use as a launch pad for an enthusiastic content strategy.

When we talk about being 'authentic', I think even by using the word we begin to step away from our true selves and start creating a version of ourselves online, one that feels close, perhaps, to the real thing, but is still trying to be an authentic version of the truth. To be really real online, you need to stop putting a barrier up between you and your audience – allowing yourself to be vulnerable and truly seen is the real way to build connection between you and your audience.

Whether you're a brand or an individual, I think truth is key. People want to engage with accounts that feel real to them, and the more honesty, vulnerability and transparency you can bring to your social media accounts, the closer your audience will feel to you. Here are a few ways that you can bring more truth online:

↪ Don't try to create a highlight reel online – show the things that haven't gone right, the bad days and mistakes.
↪ Use Instagram Stories to show the behind-the-scenes of your work.
↪ Try talking to camera to build up genuine rapport with your audience.
↪ Use IGTV and Instagram Lives as a way of answering questions and interacting with your audience.
↪ Show your personality – how can you show up for your audience in new and interesting ways?

Consistency

Look, there's no way around this: consistency is key with social media. If you're trying to build an audience, you have to show up for them. That means, however small at the start, you need to nurture your audience by being consistent with them – regular posting, replying to comments and questions, engaging on a daily basis – be present for your audience consistently. There are three main aspects of consistency on social media that are crucial:

↪ consistent posting;
↪ consistent aesthetic;
↪ consistent voice.

There is no fixed formula for consistency – some platforms benefit from you posting more often, some less. I think we can often get bogged down by the fear of the algorithms, but sometimes you just have to produce the content that you want to produce, and know that if it's good, the audience will come to you.

Consistency in attitude is also important – even when it feels like your content isn't getting the reach you want or your following isn't growing, the key is to stick at it. Here are some tips on staying consistent on social media:

↪ Create a social media schedule that feels realistic to you – however often you plan to post, do it!

↪ Know that you don't have to be everywhere – choose two platforms to focus on and try to stay consistent on those.

↪ Use social media scheduling apps like Buffer or Hootsuite if you worry consistency is an issue for you.

↪ Set yourself creativity challenges to keep your content fresh and exciting, such as a daily photo challenge.

↪ Create regular features on your social media, such as a regular time slot for an Instagram or Facebook Live or a consistent style of caption you do every week.

↪ Try not to overthink it – we often want our posts to be perfect, and that need for perfection can be crippling. Instead of perfect, try to be real, and give yourself permission to be less glossy online.

↪ Consistency also means consistent tone of voice – work out *how* you want your social media accounts to sound, not just what you want to say. Think of the language that works best with your audience and how you want your content to make them feel.

Story-telling

Social media is a narrative that you control, and by having story-driven social media accounts, you're able to take charge of that narrative and build a community around your story. People love a story; they're interested in *why* you're doing what you're doing and the story that led you to today.

We can sometimes overlook the story-telling aspect of social media when we become too fixated with the aesthetics, but the story you tell is so important. Especially with captions on Instagram, you want to draw people in with your story-telling. Here are some questions to consider to build the story-telling aspect of your social:

↪ What do you really want people to know about you and your business?
↪ What do you want them to feel when reading a caption?
↪ What journey do you want to take your audience on?
↪ What fires up your creativity? Use that as a tool for getting more creative with captions.
↪ Which accounts do you love that have story-telling at their core?

Community

Community sits at the heart of social media – without community, our platforms would be redundant. We can treat social media as if we have a megaphone to our lips, wanting to broadcast our voice and opinion to the masses. But, actually, the reverse is more beneficial – you need to *listen* on social media.

Listen to your audience, learn from them, ask them questions, respond to their comments. Community-building, in essence, is about being receptive, accessible and open – allowing people into your world and creating a space online where they feel seen and heard. When it comes to building community, here are some points to consider:

↪ Communities often grow out of your personal need. What space do you wish existed online?
↪ Is there a niche you can exploit? Being specific about who your community is for will help attract new followers to it.

↳ What groups are under-represented online? What do you personally wish to see more of?

↳ What does it mean to you to belong to a community? How does that make you feel? Try to create something that can be of service to others.

Social media: the golden rules

Soon we're going to be looking at individual platforms and how you can best serve your audience on them, but first I wanted to share some advice for questions I'm often asked. Here are my golden rules for social media:

1. You need to make yourself discoverable

Maybe an easy one, but something lots of people forget – you need to have the same handles across all platforms! Make it as easy as possible for people to find you and try to have a name that reflects you in real life. You want something that is easy to spell, with no pesky dashes or underscores.

2. You don't have to be everywhere

It's much better to do a couple of platforms well than to be everywhere. Focus on the platforms that you think would work best for your brand and create a content strategy that aims to do a few things very well.

Here are two simple questions to consider when choosing your platforms:

↳ Who are you trying to speak to, ie age, demographic, location?

↳ Where are they hanging out online?

You may love posting on Instagram, but actually your ideal client is spending more time on LinkedIn. Don't just follow the platform that you're most excited by – take some time to think about where your target audience is hanging out online.

3. You should have a call to action

Unless you're trying to monetize your social media platforms themselves, as an influencer, you want your social media to lead to something of value to your business. A powerful call to action (CTA) will give social accounts direction and focus – and also something for you to measure your growth against. Not sure what CTA your social media should have? Ask yourself what's the most valuable thing to your business right now and make that CTA your goal. Here are a few ideas:

↳ For trust-building, sending your audience to another platform builds up trust, so you could have a CTA to watch your YouTube channel and read your blog.
↳ For sales, it could be driving purchases of your product or service.
↳ For consultancy, it might be scheduling a free call or a one-to-one session.
↳ For community, you might want to drive followers to your Facebook page or newsletter.
↳ For events, you can encourage people to book tickets.
↳ For launches, you might want to tease people and get sign-ups on a waitlist.

Social media: the platforms decoded

For this section, we're going to be deep-diving into the various platforms and how you can use them to grow your business. I've enlisted the help of five social media gurus, who are experts in different channels, to share their expertise in growing online. First, let's look at everyone's favourite: Instagram.

She Made It: Instagram

Instagram is an amazing tool for female founders – it gives so much potential for visually-led companies to showcase their brand and draw in followers. Of course, it's now a very saturated platform and so making your content stand out is super important. There are some aspects to consider when perfecting your Instagram presence:

MISSION STATEMENT

What are you trying to achieve on Instagram? What's your purpose and mission statement? Having a clearly defined mission statement in mind can help guide your content strategy. For example, your mission might be to help female founders unlock their true potential through your coaching – and this can guide the content you produce. Make your mission statement – you want it to be included in your bio, along with any other stand-out information about you.

VISUALS

Instagram is obviously a visually-led platform, so making sure the visuals are on point is crucial. What you're looking for is a consistent approach to visuals, so STICK WITH A FILTER! You want people to instantly recognize your content by visuals alone, so stick to one colour palette, theme, texture and filter with images. Here are some tips on crafting visuals for Instagram:

- ↳ Create a Pinterest board where you collate your visuals – this can be used as a mood board for your Instagram, with the style of imagery you love.
- ↳ Choose a brand font and style, and stick to it! If you're using text on your Instagram, you want it to be consistent.
- ↳ Apps like VSCO are great for editing images – you can save the colour template you like and apply it to all images.

↳ Canva is fantastic for creating graphics and quotes for Instagram. You can save a brand board with all your favourite colours, which will help build a visual identity.

↳ Plan a professional photoshoot. Instagram Stories is great for behind-the-scenes, but when it comes to the main feed, people still love to see really great photography. Investing time in your imagery will serve your accounts in the long term!

VIDEO

Video is fast becoming the biggest trend on Instagram – it's a great way to put a 'face' to your business and involve your audience in a more meaningful way. If you think video content could work for you, go for it! With Instagram, it's important to always be thinking of the value you're bringing to your audience – what are they learning from you? What can you teach and advise on? What's your expertise? Instagram Lives that answer people's questions are great and these can be saved as IGTVs – one way to start with video is to post people's questions on a particular topic on Stories and then answer them in a video or on Instagram Live; this way you are directly meeting the needs of your audience and setting yourself up as an authority.

CAPTIONS

Captions are a great place to share your personality and passion – and often overlooked! Of course the visuals are important, but captions are where you get to tell your story. When crafting great captions, here are a few things to consider:

↳ Work out the key messages of your Instagram account and use them as the pillars for your content strategy. Why are people following you in the first place? Try to give back to your audience by providing useful and valuable content to them. Ask yourself: what value does this caption give my audience?

↳ If in doubt, come back to your why. Use your mission statement as inspiration for creative Instagram captions.

↳ Know who it is you're talking to and speak in their language – use vocabulary, tone and language that resonates best with your demographic.

↳ Use long captions as a way of micro-blogging on Instagram – you want to include a hook to draw people in (this might be something relatable, funny, inspiring, an awakening) and then in the main body of your caption, include something that reflects your brand purpose and close with a call to action.

↳ Don't forget hashtags! You're looking to include hashtags that have a good amount of density (between 5,000 and 20,000) for the best chance of your content being seen. You may also want to create your own unique hashtag, which is another way of chronicling your life and building community.

ENGAGEMENT

Right, so we've touched on engagement a lot in this chapter, but I want to break down exactly what I think meaningful engagement means and how to maximize it. It's not enough to have fans – you want people who are actively commenting, sharing and boosting your Instagram content – so let's try to go beyond the likes. Here's what I think you should be doing to boost your engagement on Instagram:

↳ Follow like-minded accounts on Instagram, comment and share their content.

↳ See who is regularly engaging with your Instagram Stories, or always likes your photos but doesn't comment, and see if you can build that relationship even more. Go on their page and check out their content, like and comment!

↳ Create a unique hashtag that your audience can use, so you can start to share user-generated content on your feeds.

↳ Place yourself in the conversation – look at popular hashtags in your niche and join the comments section. You're aiming to create some authority and recognition for your brand, so comment under posts that resonate with you – it's a great way to meet similar-minded people!

STORIES

Instagram Stories are a great opportunity to bring your audience in even closer – and people are consuming stories now more than ever. Here are some top tips I can share on crafting engaging Instagram stories:

↪ Try to have regular 'features' you do on your stories – this might be showing your morning coffee, daily workout or doing a Friday Q&A session. Whatever it is, regularity is key to building up an audience.

↪ Mix up the content – you're aiming for a mixture of photo and video content, not too much of one thing. If you're doing talking to camera stories, try to change the format every so often.

↪ Don't forget a call to action! Think of how you can engage your following even more. Maybe it's asking them to download your podcast or swipe up to watch a YouTube video. Remember that the more action you get your audience to make, the more trust and brand loyalty you're building with them.

↪ Use a geolocation and hashtags on your story to get more views (you can hide anything you don't want people to see under a sticker).

↪ Keep things fun and engaging – use polls and quizzes to get closer to your audience, ask them for questions and answer them directly. See stories as an opportunity to listen to your audience and gather feedback.

↪ Get a signature aesthetic – you're aiming for the same filter, colours and text style on all your stories. You want to make your stories distinctive and instantly recognizable for the audience.

↪ You want your stories to always be easy to digest, even with the sound off – use text on video stories with the key information to make them even easier to watch and engage with.

She Made It: Facebook

Facebook is an amazing platform for business owners, but it's becoming increasingly hard to stand out from the crowd on Facebook. You're fighting for attention in between personal posts and other competing brands. But, when used right, Facebook has unbelievable potential for community-building.

TOP TIPS: FIVE GOLDEN RULES FOR FACEBOOK ENGAGEMENT

To get the latest insights into Facebook for business, I asked Helen Turnbull, a social media consultant, for her top tips on boosting engagement on Facebook. Helen specializes in editorial social strategy and management, particularly for women's titles including *Fabulous*, *Stylist* and *Notebook* magazines. She says:

1 Consistency is key

In terms of type of content and regularity of posting, our feeds are already saturated and people are put off when faced with an overwhelming volume of posts. You'll be seen as spamming users, making them more likely to either not engage or worse, unfollow. That being said, don't post only one type of content, eg promotional posts. These will be much more effective when weaved into a strategy that incorporates posts that also educate and entertain – shares are the holy grail of social clout. A solid starting point is to think: if you saw X post on your News Feed, would you be inclined to share it? If the answer's no, edit it to increase that likelihood. Spending endless hours on social media has developed us all into experts in the user experience of social media.

2 Implement a comment strategy

You've done the hard work – identifying your audience/niche/brand – now you want people to engage. Engagement breeds reach which breeds more engagement, increasing the likelihood of your post being shown on the News Feed, which is the ultimate goal. People are reluctant to be the first to speak or express an opinion, especially on smaller pages. Remove this fear by directing

---

questions to users in the comments section of posts. It'll also give you a feel for their views, which can inform your content strategy.

3 Don't focus on vanity metrics

One million page likes aren't worth anything – people aren't stupid enough to think every single one is a genuine page fan – if no one is engaging with your content. Huge page numbers make it look like you've cheated growth, which illegitimates the content you've worked hard to produce. Nurture and provide for the followers you've already acquired – respond to their feedback, monitor their changing user habits and interests, listen to their needs and opinions.

4 Set up cross-page sharing partnerships

Reach out to brands and group admins of similar interest areas to help you penetrate an audience your content is yet to reach. For example – if your niche is money saving tips, reach out to bargain brands (eg Aldi, Home Bargains, etc) to ask if they'd be willing to share your posts and vice versa. You are giving them free advertising at the end of the day. This can also be applied within companies – at Fabulous (800,000 page likes), *The Sun* shared one post daily to their 3 million followers.

5 Don't underestimate the power of groups

Even if you have a highly engaged page, it's worth creating niche groups to authentically grow engaged communities, eg a parenting page can be zoned off into specific area groups – breastfeeding, mums of teenagers, sleeping tips, home-schooling help, etc, etc. The main page acts as a general homepage. Groups could also prove to be a valuable source of user-generated content as people are more inclined to share personal stories, etc, in a closed, safe environment with like-minded people. Inviting users to an 'exclusive' group prompts a positive response and makes customers feel personally valued, which reinforces their admiration of your page/brand, leading to more on- and offline recommendations. The algorithm also prioritizes highly engaged content from groups, so it's a no-brainer. All groups need nurturing just as much as your main page – consistently engaging is key and quality trumps quantity.

She Made It: other platforms

Honestly, I could write a whole book on social media strategy as there's so much to say! But I know it's pretty overwhelming, so I'm just going to share some headline thoughts on the other platforms and how you use them to boost your business:

TWITTER

Twitter is my favourite platform to use because it's great for dialogue, conversations and getting feedback! If you're looking to grow your following, I've found a couple of things really help with growth:

↳ Regularity is key for Twitter – you want to be posting multiple times a day and trying to keep the conversation up with your audience.

↳ Set yourself up as an authority – if you're an expert in something, highlight that! The accounts that do best are those that carry a certain authority and clout – titles such as CEO or founder give you authority.

↳ Don't be too general. Beyond that, you want to position yourself as an expert by focusing on one or two topics – your zones of genius – and not being too broad. With Twitter, it pays to have a focus and not try to just tweet about anything and everything.

↳ Position yourself as someone who creates opportunities for others – if you're looking to hire someone, put it on Twitter! If you see opportunities going on other people's feeds, retweet them! The more opportunities you give your audience, the more reason others have to follow you.

↳ Don't overlook the visuals. Even though Twitter is a words-based platform, visuals are still important! Use high-quality imagery to really amplify your message.

↳ Ask questions! I find my best content on Twitter is always when I ask questions and open it up to my audience. So stay curious and invite your audience into the conversation.

LINKEDIN

LinkedIn is a great platform for all business owners, especially anyone service-based who is looking to generate more clients. The same rules apply with LinkedIn as with other platforms – have a professional profile that truly reflects you, with high-quality images of you and up-to-date information. If you're looking to grow on LinkedIn, I asked Ange Loughran, a social media expert who runs the course LinkedIn Brilliance, for her top tips:

TOP TIPS: FIVE GOLDEN RULES FOR LINKEDIN ENGAGEMENT

When it comes to social media platforms, Instagram and Facebook are the playgrounds – LinkedIn is the boardroom – it's where the real deals go down! It's the easiest and quickest way to become known, liked and trusted as the expert in your field. LinkedIn is the only platform purposed for business, yet when it comes to us doing business on there it is probably one of the most feared! We have a false perception that it is a corporate, male-dominated platform for chest beating, hiring and firing.

Implement these five top tips daily to turn what could be your boring old CV-style dusty profile into an organic lead-generating sales page for your business:

1 **Use keywords** – LinkedIn is one big search engine. When setting up your profile, litter it with the keywords and phrases that your target market is searching for when they need a product or a service like the one you sell. Keywords can go into every section, even your old work history, which you can use to underpin your skills and experience for your current business.

2 **Write a great headline** – Content is king but headline is the queen – under your name your 'headline' is automatically pulled from your last job title. Edit this to talk directly to your target market and tell them who you help, how you help them and what that results in for them. Be bold. Be YOU.

3 **Three seconds** – You have three seconds to keep someone on your LinkedIn page – make sure the cover pic is a 'doing pic' . If you're a coach, have a pic of you coaching. If you're a virtual

---

assistant, have a desk-style picture. You can also use Canva to make an on-brand cover using their LinkedIn templates. Your profile pic needs to be your happy smiling page with clear eye contact. You get 2,000 characters in your 'About' section – the first two sentences need to be head turners! Encourage people to click 'see more' by telling a story, talk about why you do what you do, who you can help and a call to action.

4 **Be in the top 1 per cent** – Ninety-nine per cent of people on LinkedIn do not post there daily. If you made one post every day for five days a week, you'd be in the top 1 per cent. Repurpose your content from your blog, your best Facebook statuses or Instagram videos for LinkedIn. Write an article on there (blog) once a week talking directly to your target market with a case study, some tips, or industry=type news.

5 **Engage with purpose** – Spend five minutes each day engaging with the content of your peers, thought leaders in your industry, local business people and your target market. Don't leave two–four-word comments; get involved in the discussion by leaving value-packed comments and views. Copy and paste those comments into a document on your desktop and use as content ideas for your own profile the following week. Do that every day and you'll not only become noticed and valued, but you'll also never run out of content ideas.

PINTEREST

Pinterest can be a powerful tool for visually-led businesses and it's great for search engine optimization (SEO) too. I asked Marta Rodriguez, a digital marketing and communications specialist, for her insights on best practices for Pinterest. Marta is currently social media manager for Adria Solutions, after six years managing social media strategy for a range of e-commerce websites and creating digital strategies for small businesses in the UK and Spain.

TOP TIPS: FIVE GOLDEN RULES FOR PINTEREST GROWTH

Pinterest is the social media platform for 'window shopping' and, as such, it's best to understand it as a combination of a browser for images, like Google Images, and a social media platform. Pinterest is vital for online businesses and a priority for those businesses targeting female publics, as they are the vast majority of the Pinterest users and that's something you must keep in mind to plan your Pinterest strategy.

Here you have five tips to succeed using Pinterest for businesses:

1 **Create good content.** The Pinterest algorithm works in the same way a browser does, so make sure your content is useful and, more importantly, evergreen. You want to create pins that make sense to pin and re-pin season after season, such as guides and cheat sheets.

2 **Create visually attractive pins.** You can use Canva or Photoshop to create the most amazing pins. A tip is looking at the pins you like for inspiration and try to follow their style and composition, without losing your essence, because...

3 **You should look for your own style.** Once you've found your favourite pin designs, don't forget about your branding. If you are a boho-chic shop, your pins should match the style of your brand. If your shop is minimal, go for minimal pins. Use the colour palette of your brand as much as possible to boost brand awareness, and don't forget to include a link to your website in your pin!

4 **You should be consistent with your pinning strategy.** And I don't mean about post frequency. Make sure you post different types of content through the week, with title and meta data. If you have a professional website, make sure your business account and website are validated and you have applied for rich pins (it automatically picks up price and product name for e-commerce and titles for a blog post).

5 **Repurpose content.** Did a particular pin work well? Use that same content for a video pin and test what works the best for you. Do you want to bring loads of traffic to a particular blog post? Create a series of pins based on that topic. You can use Pinterest search ideas for inspiration on what type of content works the best for you. And then, test, test and test!

Social media: future trends

Finally, looking ahead, I thought it would be useful to highlight social media trends happening right now and how to make the most of them. I asked Hannah Tomaszewski, a content specialist at Hallam, for her thoughts on social media trends. A self-confessed word lover and creative writing graduate, Hannah has a strong passion for story-telling and all things social media and uses her experience working with clients across all sectors to create engaging and high-quality campaigns, advise on the best social and content strategies, and bring communities together online.

1. Video content will continue to dominate the market

While video has fast become the most popular content format on social media, this will only increase in the future, as the way we consume and create video content evolves. It continues to be a powerful form of marketing, allowing brands to better connect with audiences on a much more personal level, something which is only set to become more important in the future.

As social media is all about creating relationships and connecting with your audience, more open and informal video will be the key to connecting better with audiences. Similarly, live video is likely to become increasingly more popular as it helps to bridge the gap between brands and audiences, allowing for real-life interactions with real-life customers. The popularity of Q&As and more educational content will grow as brands work to win over viewers and provide more value in a more personable way.

2. Influencers will become more important, but the landscape will shift

It's no secret that trust is a huge commodity in the marketing landscape, and influencer marketing offers brands and businesses the unique opportunity to tap into already engaged audiences. But, when influencer marketing first became popular, it would be fair to say that plenty of content creators and brands would collaborate simply for exposure. However, now we're seeing a shift towards value-driven purchases and the need for greater transparency and honesty online.

The success of an influencer campaign is much more than just the number of likes and followers, and brands will continue to look beyond surface-level data, focusing instead on building strong relationships and connecting more closely with audiences. While at the moment it's common for brands to use influencers on a campaign-by-campaign basis, this will shift and longer-term partnerships will soon become the norm. Not only will this help to increase a brand's authenticity, but the longer an influencer works with your brand, the better they'll understand the tone of voice and style, which in turn will allow them to create better content that requires less editing and is more aligned with your ideals.

3. Chatbots will play a much bigger part in customer communication

It's no surprise that, in order to succeed in an increasingly digital world, brands need to go above and beyond to meet the needs of their customers and provide a more personal experience. And, while there are plenty of savvy businesses already taking advantage of chatbot and messenger capabilities in order to communicate with audiences online, this will only increase over time as technologies improve and bots become more 'human'.

Not only do chatbots help to save businesses money, but their AI capability also allows for a much faster, more intuitive customer journey. Chatbots are likely to become the first point of contact for many businesses, freeing up customer service representatives to deal with bigger issues. They will also work in predicting customer behaviour, allowing for a much more personalized experience.

The best use of chatbots will be in assisting customers in solving their own problems by offering self-support materials and interactive tutorials. Agents can then use the information found out by the AI technology to provide a personalized experience, rather than simply reading from a script.

4. Social media e-commerce will become more dominant as brands look to create shorter, more effective customer journeys

As we spend more and more time on social media platforms, the future of e-commerce is likely to take place outside of more traditional channels, and social media shopping will only grow as time goes on. Social selling not only allows brands to create more seamless omni-channel customer experiences, but also opens up more revenue streams, allowing for greater remarketing opportunities. Similarly, as social proof continues to be an important concept, a rise in user-generated content for social selling is inevitable, as people place greater emphasis on honesty and transparency. Interactive features such as visual searches and shoppable videos are also likely to increase in popularity as brands use interactive videos to demonstrate products, which is much more useful than standard static content in encouraging users to make purchases.

WORKBOOK

Q1: What is your personal mission statement? What are you trying to tell your audience about yourself on your feeds?

_____

_____

_____

_____

_____

Q2: What main platforms are you going to be focusing your attention on?

_____

_____

_____

_____

Q3: How often do you plan to post on these platforms?

_____

_____

Q4: What tone of voice will you adopt? What will your brand/ business sound like?

_____

_____

_____

_____

Q5: Will you be using video on your social media feeds, and, if so, what will the style be?

_____

_____

_____

Q6: What are you most nervous about with social media? How can you overcome those fears?

_____

_____

_____

_____

CASE STUDY She Made It: Lauren Armes

Name: Lauren Armes
Job title: Founder and CEO of Welltodo and business coach

How did the idea for Welltodo come about?

About seven years into my corporate career, I quit my secure job and moved from Australia to the UK. I thought that I would continue my goal of climbing the corporate ladder – but after a year I felt unfulfilled. It was at this time that I met an incredibly successful entrepreneur and started to imagine the possibilities for myself.

I started to research the areas in which I felt most passionate. Eventually, I landed on wellness. At the time, in 2014, it was a new trend but showed enormous potential, so I started to write about it from a business angle, hoping that it would help me land on my 'big business idea'. I soon realized that what I was doing could become the business. What started as a 'hobby blog' evolved into Welltodo, the business it is today.

How did you build up your audience on the website and social?

In 2015, Instagram was a hive of wellness activity, so it was easy to generate an audience on social media. In talking about the business of wellness (as opposed to the lifestyle), I had carved out a niche that people could sink their teeth into. The content was critical. I continued to work full-time for almost a year after launching Welltodo, but I made publishing at least four articles per week and sending a newsletter out a non-negotiable. Over time, the subscriber base and following organically grew. It came down to consistent, high-quality, highly relevant content that people weren't able to find anywhere else.

How did you monetize the platform? What are some of the challenges in monetizing digital?

It was difficult at first because the 'business of wellness' was a niche conversation. We were never going to get millions of readers. Rather than trying to build a traditional media business – that drives revenue through ads and affiliates – I launched an offline event series. This was a critical component because, again, nobody else was doing this and it created a community of 'wellness entrepreneurs' that didn't previously exist. It built immense amounts of trust and authority for the brand –

and from there I was able to dig into the needs of my audience. The revenue then began to come from partnerships (who wanted to reach our audience), consultancy services, and eventually industry-specific recruitment.

Five top tips for creating content that drives audiences?

My tips would be:

↳ Know your audience – including their pain points, their frustrations and their fears, as well as their desires and wants.

↳ Don't try and be for everybody. In doing so you end up resonating with nobody!

↳ Provide deep levels of value, but also think about how your content works as an engine for growth and revenue-generation as well.

↳ If you're just starting out, consider the benefit of both original content and also curation – that is, gathering great content from other platforms to save your audience time.

↳ Have a clear 'why' for your content – this is particularly critical if you want to build a brand with real meaning and purpose behind it.

How important is Instagram for your content strategy? Does content still have a role to play?

Instagram is critical on both an organic level and also paid. It's a commercial entity, and to fully leverage it, a paid strategy is now essential. We use it for lead-generation and to increase engagement in our free content, so that it builds a 'know, like, trust' element with our audience to ensure they see the value in our paid products too. Editorial is critical for Welltodo as an audience- and community-builder, and it is also driving lead-generation for two other companies I co-own – Welltodo Search, Tama Agency – and my own expert coaching business.

How can you use content to amplify your brand and business?

A great way of thinking about it is by looking at the word authority. It comes from the word author – which is somebody who writes (books, articles, documents, etc). Content is key to creating authority, for building trust, for creating connection, and for providing meaning behind a brand, product or service. I see it as an engine for almost any business, in telling the stories, communicating the value and expressing the purpose of the brand behind it.

Any tips for crafting your unique voice online?

Here are a few top tips:

↪ Start with knowing who you are – through deep self-exploration and personal development.

↪ Make space in your life for creative thinking – so that you don't unconsciously regurgitate somebody else's words and can find your own.

↪ Consider yourself as a contributor, not a guru – you don't need to know it all; you just need to know something.

↪ Commit to the process of finding your voice, rather than expecting it to land in your lap.

↪ Be playful and be you – it's meant to be fun!

As a coach, what do you often see holding women back from reaching their true potential?

More than anything, I believe a lot of women are stuck in fear because they don't have clarity on the next steps to take. Dale Carnegie says: 'Inaction breeds doubt and fear. Action breeds confidence and courage.' If you feel afraid, seek out a mentor and a tribe to support you with knowing the next steps forward, and go for it.

What's a quote that really inspires you?

Allowing yourself to dream as an entrepreneur, as a woman, as a human, is so powerful. Here's one of my favourite quotes: 'The number one reason most people don't get what they want is that they don't know what they want.' –T Harv Eker. Decide what you want and make a plan to get it.

CHAPTER FIFTEEN

PR strategy for your business

PR is such a powerful tool and a huge topic! In this chapter, I'll be helping you create a PR strategy for your business, work with influencers and spot media opportunities. Being both an editor and an entrepreneur for six years, I've been on both sides of PR and, as someone who gets hundreds of press releases every day, I've learned lots about what stands out to journalists! There's no secret trick to PR because, ultimately, it's about the quality of the product or service you have – the better the offering, the more legitimate and authentic your business, the more the press will come to you!

That said, there's definitely things you can do to make your business more press-worthy, and having a PR strategy can work so well with your business goals. In this chapter, we'll be looking at how to generate press interest in your business, write press releases and engage journalists in the digital age. Let's dive in.

PR strategy: why do it?

When it comes to crafting a PR strategy, I think the place to start is to question, why, exactly, you think you need PR. Here are a few questions to consider:

↪ What are you trying to achieve with PR? Is it sales, brand awareness, credibility?
↪ What customers/clients are you trying to attract with PR?
↪ What kind of publications are these target customers reading/watching?
↪ What are the short-term and long-term goals with your PR?
↪ What is the next level that you think PR will take your brand to?

PR can be powerful for both brands and individuals. For founders, it can help raise your profile, establishing you as an expert in your field, creating credibility and authority. For brands, it can help drive sales, demand and hype around your business. Depending on the level of press attention you're looking to attract, you may be able to do it yourself or you might want to take on an agency to help. I always say to founders that if you're doing all the things discussed in the book – using social media to promote your work, taking speaking opportunities and building a strong mission into your business – then press is something that will be happening organically over time! You can start doing your own PR today just by telling people far and wide about your business through all the free channels available to you.

PR strategy: what is press-worthy?

I receive hundreds of press releases every day and I can tell you, most of what gets sent to journalists doesn't even get looked at. To create a really great PR strategy, you need to think carefully about the story-telling of your brand – what story are you trying to tell the press? What's exciting and news-worthy about your business? A product launch simply isn't enough – new products are launching every day. Being a female founder isn't enough – there's more female founders now than ever! For something to be truly press-worthy, it needs to be special! Here are a few tips that will help catch the eye of a journalist:

↪ **Relevancy in the news cycle** – is there something really interesting happening in the news right now that you can tap into? Perhaps your product or service has a role to play with what's happening in the world? Could your company provide comment on particular trends?

↪ **Expert commentary** – journalists are always looking for expert commentary on news happenings – setting yourself up as an expert (as we've learned how through social media) will help position you for more media opportunities.

↪ **Data and insights** – if your company has interesting data to share, this can really help with press coverage. Perhaps you can conduct a study with your users or analyse data on the habits of your customers – anything that provides an interesting insight for journalists.

↪ **Exclusivity** – do you have something exclusive that you can offer journalists? Perhaps it's unique access to a spokesperson or a story that hasn't been covered in the press before. Journalists are always excited by a story that feels fresh and new – giving exclusive access can help sell your story.

↪ **Viral potential** – journalists are always looking for stories that have viral potential. If you've got something really unique in your story – maybe it's a sell-out product or a quirky innovation – then promote that!

PR strategy: the fundamentals

There are some fundamentals of PR that I think are really important to note. For journalists, PR plays an important role as it's how we source our stories and inspiration – without PR, there would be a lot less to write about! That said, when you're competing with hundreds of other brands for the attention of a journalist, it's crucial to understand some core principles of PR as we see it.

PR is... personal

PR is highly personal. Journalists often work with the same PRs again and again – so building up trust and credibility that you have interesting and news-worthy stories is vital. If you're doing PR for yourself, know that the more personable you can be, the more chance you have of your pitch landing.

PR is... about people

People-centric PR is always the best way to sell your story – journalists are interested in the *people* behind the businesses, so you may find that pitching interviews, expert commentary or quotes sells better than a standard press release. Try to always find the humanity in your pitch and connect with journalists on a deeper level by highlighting the *why* of any story.

PR is... about speed

I hate to say it, but often the pitch that wins is the one that gets back to you quickest. Especially with digital publications, the lead times and turnaround are very quick. If a journalist asks for a quote or imagery or more information, speed, speed, speed! Ideally you'll have everything ready in a Dropbox folder so they have everything they need already, but always be on hand quickly to help with the story!

PR is... more than press releases

It's simply not enough to send out a blanket press release and hope it gets pick-up. Like I said, PR is personal, and the more personalized you can make your pitch, the better. Take an interest in the work of a journalist, read their work and share or engage with them online – become a fan and you'll find that your pitches always get a softer landing!

PR is... purpose-driven

Like I said earlier, you need to know the purpose of the PR to measure whether it's working. If you have a purpose with your pitching, you'll have target demographics in mind and be able to tailor your pitches to the right publications. You don't want to have a woolly strategy – make it purpose-driven and then you have something to measure your success against!

PR is... about creating your own luck

Okay, so, look, there's no smoke without fire. If you're looking to get press coverage, you have to do something interesting. Whether that's launching your own festival, creating an amazing podcast or creating a world-first product, innovation is really where PR begins. Don't try to go after press too early – you need some proof of your concept/hard work/success, and then you're in a great position to get press. I see it often with brands when they first launch – they want all the press hype about their launch, but actually they don't have that many stockists or sales yet. Try not to rush into the press angle – sometimes holding off until you've got something really interesting to show is a much better route for success.

PR strategy: how to get media opportunities

There are several ways you can gather media opportunities and get coverage – here are a few ideas of different ways to work with journalists:

1 **Send out a press release** – a succinct press release for anything news-worthy can be great for your business, although it's not always relevant. Wondering whether a press release is right for

you? Press releases tend to work best for product or brand launches, a new restaurant opening, travel news or anything ground-breaking. On the whole, I always think a more tailored approach works, so only send out a press release if you want to shout about something new to lots of people at once!

2 **Send an email pitch** – the best way to get media coverage in my eyes is to send out a tailored email pitch to journalists with your story. I'll explain more below on best practice for pitching on email!

3 **Pitch yourself for podcasts** – podcasts are such a great way to promote yourself and they are an ever-growing medium! Find podcasts that are really relevant and popular in your sector, industry or niche and take an interest in them. Comment on their social media, engage with their host. Build rapport with the podcast host and producer, and why not pitch yourself as a guest?

4 **Approach broadcast producers** – broadcast opportunities can be so great for businesses, and if you've got a particular expertise or interesting commentary to make, the producers would love to hear from you! Broadcast often works at much greater speed than traditional print and digital media, so you'll have to be very on the ball to get these opportunities. My advice would be to follow TV and radio producers on Twitter (you can find them through search) and always look out when they are looking for someone to provide commentary. You'll find that once you've done a few broadcast opportunities, it will be much easier to build more as producers love working with the same people again and again!

5 **Check the #journorequest hashtag on Twitter** – the #journorequest hashtag is what journalists will often use when they are looking for interesting information or case studies for a story. Be quick as these chances often move fast, but it can be a great way of introducing yourself to journalists and creating more opportunities for yourself.

6 **Follow journalists on Twitter** – such a simple one, but the more journalists and editors you follow and engage with on Twitter, the more chance of media opportunities you have! I think trying to build rapport with journalists on social media *before you need them* is a great place to start. Showing you take an active interest in their writing conveys genuine enthusiasm and, also, it's flattering! Flattery gets you a long way in the media industry.

7 **Sign up to ResponseSource, Cision and Press Plugs** – there are loads of great media resources where journalists will post what stories they are working on and you can get in touch. Sign up to all the relevant newsletters to make sure you hear of all the opportunities.

PR strategy: what you need before approaching press

There's no magic formula to PR; however, there are certain things you must have at your disposal that will help you if an opportunity arises. Before approaching the press, here's a check-list of things you must have:

↪ **A press release** – you don't need to send it out, but it's useful to have one on file. I've written a handy guide below on how to write a great press release.

↪ **High-res imagery** – this is a *must*. You need really great quality imagery for your pitch – ideally you'll have professional photos of both yourself and your product/service. Make sure you have photos in both portrait and landscape, so there's a range of options available.

↪ **A list of stockists** – if it's a product business, a list of stockists is a good idea.

↪ **Any stats/figures** – a journalist may want stats to back up your claims. Keep a list of any key information about the success of your business that can support your pitch.

↪ **Testimonials** – if you're a service business, I think it's always good to have testimonials on hand. If you're trying to build your authority, testimonials are a great way to highlight your expertise.

↪ **Quotes ready** – of course you'll want to create tailored quotes for a particular story, but I think having quotes on hand about yourself, your product or offering is really useful. It might be the thing that helps sell your story, so have a few things saved that you can whip out!

↪ **A Dropbox with everything a journalist needs** – I would put your high-res imagery and press release together in a Dropbox folder, so the journalist can have easy access to it.

PR strategy: how to write a winning press release

Press releases can be a useful way of getting all the key information about your business on one page. I find most press releases can be a little overdone, so here are my top tips on writing a great press release:

↪ Keep it short – most press releases I get are super long-winded. You really want to keep it as short as possible, include all the relevant information and convey the real 'story' here, but don't overdo it.

↪ Make sure to include social media handles, website URL and any key information, such as addresses, RRP, launch date or embargoes.

↪ Include a high-res landscape photo – this can help give your press release personality and vibrancy.

↪ Include a 'Notes to Editors' section at the end that includes the most important information and highlight this in bold.

↪ Don't use overly flowery language or too many adjectives. It always seems a little 'PR-y' when everything is 'incredible' and 'innovative' and 'extraordinary'. Try to imagine that the person reading it knows nothing about your business and you don't want to overdo it with the hyperbolic language, otherwise it comes across as a little fake and pushy!

PR strategy: how to send out a great email pitch

My advice for anyone trying to get press coverage is to send out cold emails to journalists with your story. We're used to receiving unsolicited emails all day from individuals, so honestly, if you're nervous about doing it, I say just go for it! There are definitely some dos and don'ts for approaching journalists, though, so here are my tips for how to send out a great email pitch that is likely to land coverage:

↪ **Personalize the first line** to every journalist you email – ideally, I'd say target each email to the individual publication and tailor your pitch accordingly, but if you're not able to do that, make sure to personalize the first line at least with their name!

↪ **Give their social media a stalk before** – can you say something friendly and personal in the first line? Perhaps they've recently been on holiday to Italy or they've written an article which you loved reading. Say something complimentary and personal in the first paragraph to show you take genuine interest in their work and life.

↪ **Keep your pitch short** – all you need to do is send a very short summary of your story and offer to send more information. This only needs to be three to four lines and should contain all the key information of the story, including any stats, facts or accolades. Whether you're pitching a news story, an interview, case study or product, you need to keep it succinct and interesting.

↪ **Offer to send over more information** – you can attach a press release to the email or follow up with high-res imagery or quotes. If you're offering, though, make sure to send it quickly when they say yes!

↳ **Don't chase too soon** – if you don't hear anything back, wait two days before sending a follow-up email. Most journalists are very busy and aren't ignoring you on purpose, promise!

PR strategy: how to make yourself stand out as a founder

Want to create more media opportunities for yourself as founder? There are a few things you can do that really highlight your press-worthiness and boost your profile:

1 **Create a one-page media profile** – a one-page PDF that contains all the key information on your personal profile, including any stand-out credentials, accolades or expertise, is super handy. You can use this to pitch journalists, event organizers and attach to your LinkedIn profile. Make sure to include a professional high-res photo of you on it to make it shine!

2 **Apply for awards** – awards are a great way to build credibility for yourself or your business. Find out what awards are going in your industry and apply, apply, apply! Industry-specific awards are also a really great way to build your authority in a particular niche.

3 **Pitch for speaking opportunities** – speaking opportunities are a great way to build your profile. You may want to reach out to event and festival organizers on LinkedIn and pitch yourself as a speaker. Make sure to get a video recording of any speaking you do, as this can be really useful for later! Panel events are another great way to raise your profile – look on Eventbrite for interesting events in your industry and get in touch with the organizer.

4 **Create your own speaking opportunities** – why not create your own media opportunities? You could launch your own networking breakfast, small event or even launch a festival. Sometimes you have to create your own magic, and I've found the more of our own events I've hosted, the more I've been approached for speaking opportunities with others!

5 **Do a TEDx talk** – if you've got a burning story to tell, why not apply to do a TEDx talk. They are an amazing way to boost your profile! You can ask someone to nominate you as a speaker or suggest yourself as a speaker. The TEDx events are independently organized and they are often looking for amazing speakers with an interesting entrepreneurship story to tell.

6 **Start a podcast** – maybe an obvious one, but if you're looking to position yourself as a thought leader, a podcast is a great place to start! It's a fantastic way to network with other like-minded individuals by inviting them on to your show and it really helps put a face – and voice – to your work. Podcasting has become a very competitive space, so I would encourage you to think outside the box and think of an interesting format, niche or collaboration that would make the show stand out against others in a similar space.

WORKBOOK

Q1: What have you learned that you're trying to achieve with PR?

_____

_____

_____

_____

Q2: How will you measure the success of your PR campaign?

_____

_____

_____

_____

Q3: What main ways are you going to approach journalists?

_____

_____

_____

_____

Q4: What kind of media opportunities are you looking for? What do you think will best benefit your business and career right now?

_____

_____

_____

_____

Q5: What steps do you now need to take to create a PR strategy for your brand?

_____

_____

_____

_____

CASE STUDY   She Made It: Natalie Trice

Name: Natalie Trice
Job title: Author and award-winning PR coach

Where do you start when it comes to building a PR strategy for your business?

I think that the place to start is by understanding that PR is not free advertising. PR is a powerful way to build your business, position yourself as an expert and to be seen as a media go-to, and that is priceless. Get an understanding of what it is you're looking for:

- Look at what being on the pages of magazines and newspapers could do for you.
- Or do you want to be on podcasts and IG squares?

Whatever it is, PR is a personal recommendation where someone else is talking about you and giving you access to their audience, and that is pretty amazing.

Look at what you want to gain from PR, see what you are doing now and go from there.

What does good PR look like to you?

Good PR to me is when an individual or brand is seen in key media outlets on an ongoing basis, using the same strong messaging and being a part of the conversation.

From the NHS and Sir Captain Tom, to Joe Wicks and Florence Given, people are out there doing amazing things with PR and it speaks volumes.

The thing with PR is that you don't have to spend a fortune, but you do have to keep at it.

I tell people who do my courses and workshops to do something small each day, and as you flex your PR muscle, things will happen.

Essentially I see PR as a way to put you in the spotlight, for the right reasons, to let people know who you are and what you do and to become a leader in your field. You could be a yoga teacher, business coach, baker or florist, whatever it is – PR lets people know you are out there and ready to work with them.

Do you need to take on an agency to handle your PR or can you do it yourself?

I am not talking anyone out of a job, but you can do your own PR. I have written PR School, which is a masterclass in self-publicity.

I think it is like many things in a business: do you have time to do it, do you understand what you need to do and can you get it done? In the early days, it might be that you need to do your own PR and can make it absolutely manageable. Having a decent website and social media channels is a good starting place, as well as having a list of five publications where you want to be seen and these are the places where your target audience hang out!

As the coverage comes in and you start to get a media presence, it might be that you want to take on a consultant, but when that time comes, do your research, find the right fit for you and brief them!

What are your five top tips for securing press coverage?

↪ It is a marathon, not a sprint, so know from the start you are in it for the long haul.

↪ Be polite – the press are helping you, so always get them what they want, when they want, and if they help you, say thanks – you will be amazed at how many people don't do that!

↪ Be fast and prepared – I would suggest having a strong biography and head or product shots at the ready if someone wants them and make it easy for people to find you. The number of times I have left a website as I can't find an email address is off the scale – be in it to win it!

↪ Work out where you want to be and if it's going to help with your overall business goals! Yes, being in *Psychologies* is amazing, but make sure it is aligned with your why and is part of an overall strategy.

↪ Have good images! A picture paints a thousand words and there is no reason in this mobile phone age why you can't have them taken and ready to send out. I even managed to have Zoom photos taken during lockdown – if you want this to be a success, you will find a way.

What makes a great story, in your eyes?

Think about what you are actually trying to say and what it is that you want it to achieve. A new shop opening last year might have not been news, but post-COVID-19, it could be seen as bold and brave and make a great story. People want to know about people, about success, about triumph over tragedy, so think: what does this story tell?

And last of all, look at the places you want to be seen and work out where you might fit!

Any tips for writing a great press release?

In a nutshell = eye-catching headline, short, to-the-point paragraphs, approved quotes, contact details and images.

Some people say that the press release is dead, but I still think that if it contains news and you send it to the right people, it can be the start of a conversation and a new relationship, and that's so important.

Any dos and don'ts when approaching journalists?

YES! Do your research. If you are making cat beds, don't send the details to a journalist who loves dogs.

Get their name right – I hate being called Nats, Nathalie, and 'hun' – and I know I am not the only one.

If you are sending out a press release, don't then put your out of office on and go on holiday. If you want people to talk about you, you want them to do it for all the right reasons, so be around to help them if they do show interest.

I tend to send information out via email. Not all PR people do this, and some journalists like the phone, but don't send an email and then phone them to ask if they have it.

Leave the kisses at the end of emails for your mum, not the features editor of *Red*!

How is PR changing thanks to social media? Any advice on getting coverage with influencers?

I talk a lot about being your own media maker. I started out in PR when fax machines were the height of technology and when an editor's red pen was the only way to be visible.

Today you can be online in moments on your own feeds, but with influences and online outlets, you can send a story out at 10am and be out there within the hour.

Now is not the time to stand back and let others take the limelight – there is so much opportunity out there, if you are hungry for it, you get to be part of the picture.

Should you have to give any free product to secure coverage?

This has to be done on a case-by-case basis. There are times when, yes, you really do, and if it means your healthy recipe book is reviewed in *Health & Fitness* or your custom sweatshirts are in the *Grazia* gift guide, YES! If a small blogger who posts once a month wants an all-inclusive week in your hotel, I think not!

See how important it is to you, the value you would get from it, and make a judgement call.

CHAPTER SIXTEEN

Supercharge your community with events

In this final chapter of *She Made It*, we're going to be looking at how you can supercharge your business by building a lively community in real life. As we've learned, community-building is vital for businesses, especially female-owned business, where there's huge potential to bring women together over shared goals, interests and challenges. In my years of running About Time, I've learned so much about in-person dialogue and growing your audience – I can't wait to reveal my secrets for supercharging your business through events. Let's get stuck in!

Events 101: everything you need to know

Live events are a powerful tool for supercharging your relationship with your audience. Through our #SheStartedIt LIVE festivals, we've been able to speak directly to the women who follow us on social media and engage with our content regularly – getting that feedback face-to-face has been invaluable, and it's only strengthened our bond, connection and understanding with our audience. Putting together an in-person event for your audience is such a great way to supercharge your community and really add value to your offering. Here are some questions to consider when planning events:

→ **Where does an event fit with your brand's mission statement?** How can you use live events to further the purpose of your business and work? For example, I am passionate about promoting female entrepreneurship, and empowerment is one of my core values – our festival #SheStartedIt LIVE was a natural evolution from my podcast #SheStartedIt (which also led to this book!) – we had begun to build a community of aspiring female entrepreneurs around us through the business, and a live event created a deeper way for women to connect and network face-to-face.

→ **What kind of event and timing would work best for your audience?** We found that for our audience, after-work events weren't ideal as many of them had childcare responsibilities. Weekend events work best for our audience and we were able to put on complimentary childcare, so that they could bring their little ones too!

→ **Are you going to charge for your event?** If so, try to create a price point that is accessible for everyone. We also always give away free spaces to anyone who can't afford to come – accessibility is key! Figure out a price point that works for both you *and* your audience – you still want to make a profit on your event, so see if there's any costs you can cut down on to bring the ticket price down whilst still offering a great event to your audience.

→ **How can you reach a bigger audience?** Perhaps you'd like to also live-stream your event on Facebook or Instagram or make a video recording that will be available after the event.

Top tips: selling out your events

Everyone wants their live event to sell out! It's basically the goal, right? Of course, you need to put on a quality event with a great line-up, but there are definitely some tricks of the trade that can help your event sell out:

↳ **Make your event easy to find** – you want your event to be search-engine-friendly, whatever platform you use. Make sure that the event title contains the keywords for the audience you're trying to attract. I would create a specific hashtag for the event too, so you can keep an eye on any user-generated content surrounding the event.

↳ **Speak in terms of your audience** – want to make your event really enticing? For the copy, you need to think in terms of your audience – what are they gaining from coming? What will they learn? Who is the event for? Make the event copy short and sassy – but, most importantly, highlight exactly why they should be booking a ticket to this event! You want to convey a sense of urgency, so you may want to offer early bird tickets to make it feel even more exciting.

↳ **Create a varied social media strategy** – think carefully about a content strategy for your event. You need to develop a plan that means you're not repeating yourself but still driving sales – think of different aspects of the event you can highlight in the lead-up, such as profiling any speakers involved, the food on offer or testimonials of previous attendees. A lively social media strategy means reinforcing the same message (BUY NOW!) but finding new and interesting ways to talk about it.

↳ **Tease your audience** – I always advise with events not to give away everything at the start. With our festivals, we'll have upwards of 40 speakers on the day – I've found that announcing a few headline speakers at the launch of the festival and then drip-feeding new speakers in the lead-up works well to build momentum. You don't want to give away all the information on the launch day; keep some things back so you can always have something fresh to talk about on social media!

↪ **Use paid social marketing** – I haven't talked about paid marketing a lot in this book because, honestly, I think the best social media is all organic! That said, when it comes to events you have a very clear ROI, as you're trying to sell tickets, so it's quite easy to measure the impact and reach of paid spend. I've found paid spend on Instagram for events can be really effective, especially alongside a great email marketing strategy.

↪ **Focus on your email marketing** – newsletters are obviously a great way to promote your event, but I think you need to be considering what unique value you can give to your audience who sign up to your newsletter. This might be a special discount code, an exclusive interview with one of the speakers or early access to tickets – if you're looking to drive newsletter sign-ups, you have to think of the value you're adding to your subscribers!

↪ **Make sure you've got great, consistent event imagery** – the visuals with events are so important! Canva have some great templates you can use for your events – but like I said on general content strategy, keep the imagery consistent with the same brand colours, fonts and styles.

↪ **Do tiered ticket pricing** – tiered ticket pricing is another great way of enticing your audience. Create exciting offers, such as early bird discounts, to try to maximize sales at launch. We've found a bring-a-friend-for-free offer works really well for us – not only are you getting an extra person attending, but often their friend will be like-minded and your community will be naturally growing!

↪ **Consider the reach of your speakers** – one of the best ways we've grown our events is by bringing in speakers who have their own social following. It's not enough to rely on your channels alone – after a while, you'll find you're just speaking to the same people again and again. By bringing in speakers to your events, you're casting a wider net of fans and followers who'd like to come and your reach will automatically grow! Think of speakers who have a different audience from yours (age, demographic, location) but are interested in similar topics.

↳ **Think of brand partners who can elevate your event** – brand partnerships are another great way to boost the profile of your events. What are you looking for in a brand partner? A brand who shares similar values to you, who can connect with your audience and bring life to your event.

↳ **Remember, you've got a captive audience!** You've got such a captive audience with events – make the most of it! Try to find time on the day to speak to your audience, get feedback, ask them questions and generally interact with them. What's more, you can send tailored feedback forms after the event, so you can make it even better for the next one – don't forget to collect email addresses on the day for this. Testimonials can form a powerful part of a future social media strategy, so great testimonials will be so useful for building the potential of your events.

EXPERT GUIDE: HOW TO MAKE YOUR EVENT INCREDIBLE

The thing about events is … they're not just evenings, days, happenings that take place and then they're over. Events are moments and memories – they have an incredible superpower of connecting people, brands, products, messages, celebrations and more. And as an entrepreneur, harnessing this superpower can really level up whatever it is you do; helping you reach a greater audience, rewarding your community and celebrating in the moments together.

Everyone has the potential to create events, but I want to share some of my tips to create incredible events – with 10 years in the industry and a whole lot of hustle and heart poured in, I truly live and breathe this world and am a huge advocate for what events can do to elevate any business.

So, what makes an incredible event? An incredible event is one that your guests carry on talking about long beyond event day – for the right reasons! They've told their friends and family, they've posted about it on their socials and, most importantly: they are on the lookout for your next one.

But how can you make your events stand out from the crowd and truly shine?

Getting started is all about knowing your why. Set strategic goals for every event that you plan, even if it's the first event you've ever put together. Know exactly what its purpose is, who your attendees are, what kind of events they already go to and what they want to see from you.

Make your objectives SMART (specific, measurable, achievable, relevant, time-based) and keep them at the core of your planning throughout the process. Don't just plan events because you feel like everyone is planning events (this stands for virtual too!) – have goals that you can work towards, because then your purpose will pour into every corner of your event.

This leads me on to the attendee journey. I'm not just talking about how they'll physically arrive at your event, but the entire process. From the moment that invitation drops on their doorstep, into their inbox, or they see your event announcement on your latest Instagram post – is the excitement building and is your event's core purpose singing through every single word they read?

Weave the theme of your event through the journey the attendee will take – through the RSVP or booking page, to the reminders and lead-up, to when they arrive at the door. Is your brand fun and exciting? Make sure your guests are met with fun and excitement! I'm talking hosts wearing brand colours and big smiles, experiential surprises and Instagrammable moments. Continue to think about all the touchpoints your guests will meet along the way.

Be like a swan. Appear calm on the surface but paddle like crazy underneath! The key to *appearing* like you've got it together on event day is just this. You can be tearing your hair out over misplaced deliveries, extra guests turning up, an unexpected VIP or tube strikes making everyone late. But the difference between someone organizing an event and an event organizer is that we know how to be calm. Because if we're confident and calm, our guests will be in our abilities, too. (Think flight attendants during extreme turbulence.)

I really encourage you, on event day, as the doors are about to open and the excitement is rising, to just take a moment. Whatever the event – its size, its purpose – YOU have created it. You've created an opportunity for people to come together to share an experience – it might be the experience of your brand or a celebration for a pivotal moment in your entrepreneurial career. But it's a memory to cherish. So stand back, take a look around, take a photo, take a deep breath – you've got this!

WORKBOOK

Q1: What kind of events would work best with your community?

_____

_____

_____

_____

Q2: What other experts and speakers can you bring into your events?

_____

_____

_____

_____

Q3: What brands align best with yours that could be great brand partners?

_____

_____

_____

_____

Q4: What kind of social media strategy will you adopt for your event?

_____

_____

_____

_____

Q5: What is the purpose of hosting events for you? Is it money, community, brand-strengthening? Get clear on what you're trying to achieve with your events.

_____

_____

_____

_____

Conclusion

I really hope through the pages of this book that you have found inspiration, clarity, focus and drive. There's so much potential for female entrepreneurship to boom, and with the right tools, resources and systems in place, I really think that women are unstoppable.

I'd like to leave you with one final piece of advice: if you need support, look within your network. There is no better place to find resilience, strength and kinship than through the power of sisterhood. Support other women – be generous with your networks, share your advice, and remember it's not about fighting for seats at the top, but creating more seats. We need to go beyond words and show our sisterhood with actions now.

Whatever life and business throws at you, I hope you know how strong and capable you really are. Day by day, month by month, you're setting a new standard for women everywhere and showing the magic of what happens for a woman when she believes in herself. For our generation and the next, you're creating something amazing. Remember that good days and bad days will come, but the sun still rises every day – and you have the potential to start again.

What you create today will have a ripple effect for years to come. Your self-belief today creates a new normal for women tomorrow – go out and dream.

Notes

Preface

1 Rose A (2019) [accessed 4 August 2020] *The Alison Rose Review of Female Entrepreneurship 2019* [online] https://assets.publishing. service.gov.uk/government/uploads/system/uploads/attachment_data/ file/784324/RoseReview_Digital_FINAL.PDF (archived at https:// perma.cc/3JY8-DWMA)

Chapter One

1 NatWest Group (2019, March 19) [accessed 5 September 2020] *NatWest launches 'Back Her Business' – a female-only crowdfunding programme [online]* https://www.rbs.com/rbs/news/2019/03/natwest-launches-back-her-business--a-female-only-crowdfunding-p.html (archived at https://perma.cc/KA4S-MEGW)

Chapter Two

1 *Estée Lauder: The Sweet Smell of Success* (1987) A+E Networks
2 Smith, Z (2006) *On Beauty*, Penguin, London

Chapter Three

1 Rose A (2019) [accessed 4 August 2020] *The Alison Rose Review of Female Entrepreneurship 2019* [online] https://assets.publishing. service.gov.uk/government/uploads/system/uploads/attachment_data/ file/784324/RoseReview_Digital_FINAL.PDF (archived at https:// perma.cc/AD5W-WFDV)

Chapter Seven

1 The Pipeline (2020) [accessed 10 August 2020] *WOMENCOUNT2020: Role, value, and number of female executives in the FTSE 350* [online] https://www.execpipeline.com/wp-content/uploads/2020/07/The-Pipeline-Women-Count-2020-FINAL-VERSION.pdf (archived at https://perma.cc/TPM3-JG3H)

2 The Pipeline (2020) [accessed 10 August 2020] *WOMENCOUNT2020: Role, value, and number of female executives in the FTSE 350* [online] https://www.execpipeline.com/wp-content/uploads/2020/07/The-Pipeline-Women-Count-2020-FINAL-VERSION.pdf (archived at https://perma.cc/T72F-TV9C)

3 *The Telegraph* (2009, April 2) [accessed 7 September 2020] G20 Summit: Michelle Obama tells children they are future world leaders [online] https://www.telegraph.co.uk/news/worldnews/michelle-obama/5096908/G20-summit-Michelle-Obama-tells-children-they-are-future-world-leaders.html (archived at https://perma.cc/8DL9-9NB6)

Index

Note: Case studies, top tips *and* workbooks are indexed as such.

Printed in the USA
CPSIA information can be obtained
at www.ICGtesting.com
LVHW061631180923
756757LV00056B/383

9 781789 666847